Students and Extern.

# TREASURY RULES

# Treasury Rules

## Recurrent Themes in British Economic Policy

## Adrian Ham

Quartet Books

London   Melbourne   New York

First published by Quartet Books Limited 1981
A member of the Namara Group
27/29 Goodge Street, London W1P 1FD

ISBN 0 7043 2267 6

Phototypeset by
Trendsetter, Brentwood, Essex

Printed in Great Britain
by Mackays of Chatham Ltd

For Kathy

# Contents

# Preface

This book was written to make some general criticisms of civil servants and the way their world and ideas affect politicians and therefore policy. No remarkable elixir or nostrum is offered to solve what is, in the author's belief, an urgent national problem. Some people will feel that the way that HM Treasury has been portrayed betrays an unusual bitterness towards civil servants at the senior level. I hope that it will become clear that I feel they are playing out the role which they believe is their prerogative, and which fits in with their culture and perception of the world. That I fundamentally disagree with that perception will be obvious. Nevertheless, I know very well from my own experience in the Treasury that there are many sensible, well-intentioned officials of great intelligence in senior positions. If there are villains in the sad economic drama that has unrolled over recent decades, they are the doctrines that have bedevilled British economic policy-makers. When consideration is given to the economic record, the comfortable belief that, as a nation, we are pragmatic and practical in policy matters seems eminently false. The recrudescence of vulgar monetarism in the late seventies has surely laid the myth to rest.

Without great encouragement from my wife Kathy, I am sure that this work would not have been completed, crammed, as it was, into odd corners of a rather busy existence.

I am most grateful to Lord Balogh, whose own works and comments have been a great source of encouragement for my

ix

efforts. I also have to thank Francis Cripps, Barry Davis and Paul Ormerod for their helpful criticism. They carry no responsibility for what has resulted, of course. I have enjoyed the magnificent facilities of the new Public Record Office building at Kew (many references are given in the standard Public Record Office format), and must express thanks to Wynn Godley at the Department of Economic Affairs at Cambridge for giving me use of facilities there, and to my father, Thomas Ham, for some most useful research in the Bodleian Library at Oxford. I am also most grateful to Paul Cox, Bob Redgate and Adrian Furzer for help with graphics, and to Anne McFarlane and Dorothy Culshaw for invaluable help typing.

# 1

# An Introduction

*Our grandfathers believed, with the unquestioning certainty of a religious faith, in* laissez-faire. *They held that, in economic matters, the State had only to keep out of the ring to ensure the best results. 'Private enterprise' would do all that was needed...In these days, that simple faith has been eclipsed. Our fathers were much less certain of it than our grandfathers, and in our own day it is held at all only by way of obstinate reaction against the prevailing conditions.*

*G.D.H. Cole,* Practical Economics, *1937*[1]

Since 1974, a remarkable degeneration in the formation of British economic policy has taken place. This has been closely associated with what has been hailed by some as the 'monetary revolution' and by others as a return to old values and 'sound' money. The approach to economic management in the late 1970s and early 1980s more closely resembled the application of the old-fashioned Treasury rules of the 1920s than at any time in the fifty preceding years. The phenomena associated with this violent throw-back have been the

1

stagnation and decline of Britain's vital manufacturing sector, the addition of one and a half million individuals to the dole queue, and a decisive decline in the standard of public services enjoyed by the mass of the populace. All of this, despite the discovery and exploitation of the massive national resources of oil and gas from the North Sea over exactly the same period.

How has Britain contrived to snatch economic failure from the jaws of success? To answer this question, we could examine events in various economic and political categories, almost in isolation from one another and from the broader historical context. Their roots, however, go very deep indeed, and relate to long-run trends in British economic development and in British political institutions. Consideration of events in the period between the two World Wars invites the conclusion that we are reliving a tragic period of our own history, without having learnt much or anything from the first experience. If policy were entirely determined by rash, hot-headed politicians, elected on the basis of violent public reaction against each successive radical stance, and if the executive was being constantly changed in line with swings in policy, such a full circle would be unremarkable. But few radical platforms have been overwhelmingly supported by the electorate over the past fifty years, and our Civil Service machinery has a greater continuity than any in the industrial world.

This very continuity of personnel, culture and attitude in the economic policy-making machinery is a central problem. The Treasury and the Bank of England have had a remarkable degree of autonomy and influence on politicians and for long stretches of time have set the pattern of government for the whole Civil Service apparatus. Indeed, their particular interaction with politicians has, I believe, lent itself to the recurrent failure of both major political parties to deal effectively with fundamental problems.

In the early to mid nineteenth century, when Britain was the preeminent world economic power, economic management was relatively unimportant. The profitability of much new industry was high, innovation was rapid and the opportunities for trade and markets world-wide were apparently boundless. Jobs in manufacturing expanded rapidly, as did jobs in related service industries. There were sharp business cycles, but the needs of industrialists were simply that government should not take actions which directly damaged their interests, or denied them a secure system of finance.

With currency of paper or gold, and with no specific objectives for growth or money supply, the economy as a whole tended to prosper.

The emergence of massive industrial powers abroad changed this picture. The halcyon days of free trade, free enterprise and ever-accelerating wealth for the great mass of the British people were over, as one by one major industries found themselves challenged and in many cases overtaken by industries in Europe and elsewhere.

Up to this time, the role of the civil servant had been relatively simple, particularly on the economic side. Walter Bagehot – the prominent Victorian author and political commentator – had a picture of the relationship between the official and the politician which was particularly apposite for the 'golden age' when Britain was the Workshop of the World. Then the politician was the unquestioned captain of the ship of state, and the official was merely a helmsman who converted political decisions into moment-by-moment actions.

Bagehot's framework for analysing the process of government nevertheless remains an excellent basis for considering the situation up to the present day, and Chapter 2 sets out to examine what light is shed by this approach on the nature of today's 'permanent politicians' as the Senior Civil Service has been called. The distinction which Bagehot made between the public show of government and the private reality seems as appropriate to the situation as it was in his time, although the 'public show' has spread downwards in layers to include that which was private in his day. Another important factor is the social position of civil servants. An understanding of the cohesive nature of Civil Service thought and advice necessitates some consideration of the senior civil servant as a special social case. Evidence points to an excessively in-bred society, insulated by an unusual degree of job security and high living standards from the plight of many British industries, businessmen and workers. The need to stay inside Whitehall's labyrinth for career success blinkers this new élite. These social aspects of the 'mandarins' are considered in Chapter 3. It seems clear that as Britain's economy has declined, the social eminence and prestige of its permanent administrators has increased.

At the same time, it is evident that their disdain for their political 'masters' has become less well concealed in recent years. Who could deny that some politicians were and are worthy of disdain or even contempt? But on the other hand, could we expect the permanent administrators to do better, or to be more sensitive to Britain's needs from their cosseted niches in Whitehall?

Bagehot emphasized the tendency of closed bureaucracies to harbour beliefs and doctrines well beyond the time that such tenets cease to be relevant. Because of the Official Secrets Act, it is impossible to trace the development, year by year, of fashions in economic doctrine from the late 1940s to the present day inside the Treasury corridors. The author's experience afforded only a brief window on the state of the Treasury mind from 1974 to 1976. But this period can now, with hindsight, be identified as a climacteric for the benevolent influence of Keynes on the economic decision-making process. The atavistic forces of crude monetarism and economic defeatism were hovering in the wings, waiting for their moment. To quote Samuel Brittan:

> Harrod points out that one of Keynes's most persistent themes was that we must not allow full employment policy to be impeded by balance of payments considerations. Lord Keynes would have liked both Free Trade and full employment, but he never deviated from the doctrine that full employment came first. Harrod has convincingly argued that 'the failure to achieve the full growth potential of the economy, thereby losing year by year a growing amount of wealth that could be produced' is a crying evil involving similar wastes to pre-war unemployment. 'There is a great wide world of suffering humanity whose lot could be improved if only the US and Britain raised their production to their true potential.' The provisional answer to Harrod's question about whether the Treasury has really been converted to Keynes is in techniques, yes (more than Harrod acknowledges), but in basic belief and approach, no.
>
> To be absolutely sure of the answer to this question one would need to see how the Treasury would react to high unemployment at a time when sterling was really weak. But the un-Keynesian belief of some leading Treasury men that there is little the Government could do to secure full employment in the face of adverse world forces, is not encouraging.[2]

As Harrod indicated, the pre-war economic management of the nation generated a massive volume of waste and human misery. The working of the Treasury mind during that period of social trauma is therefore of great importance, since we have clear indications of the continuity of its influence even into the economic malaise following 1976. The pre-war victory of Treasury doctrine over common sense in 1925 is discussed in Chapter 4 under the glamorous title of 'Gold Fever'. This chapter serves a double purpose, since the now-discredited logic behind that ill-fated return to the Gold Standard has since been exhumed, sponged down, and clad in fashionable monetarist clothes. The arguments posed for it, its consequences and first demise in 1931 are all, therefore, of considerable current interest. The fact that it had failed, and that its logical system was faulty, seemed to elude the pre-war Treasury, which continued to apply the classical arguments for its restoration even as the economy started once more to prosper – without the Gold Standard.

Resistance to rearmament on any scale was a logical consequence of Treasury thinking and the high point in achieving the dream of senior Treasury officials, of the Treasury as a super-ministry, was reached in the politically shameful years of the late 1930s. Development of the fleet and army was held back by the Treasury although development of greater strength for the RAF was eventually conceded. Treasury arguments were frequently used in support of the appeasement policies.

Chapter 5 discusses the role of the Treasury doctrine at this time, and the growing awareness among politicians that, after all, men and skills were what mattered not abstract financial rectitude.

The Second World War marked a total eclipse of classical monetarism and the *laissez-faire* doctrine. Even in the post-war world, it was clear that many civil servants were amenable to economic planning. Even prominent Conservatives had begun to advocate it in the late 1920s. While the period of the first post-war Labour government marked great economic progress, it nevertheless witnessed a retreat from the opportunities which were offered by a more closely controlled economy.

Chapter 6 examines some aspects of this retreat, and sketches out the sad deterioration of Britain's relative economic position from the early 1950s to 1972. Since 1951 economic planning in Britain has been a topic of discussion and the subject of at least one government White Paper, but of no real action. It has been on the agenda several times, but never reached. Meanwhile, in other countries, long-term economic planning and industrial intervention has apparently worked in mixed economies – economies with large and vigorous private sectors. The British Civil Service, on the other hand, has distanced itself from both economic planning developments abroad and the growing industrial problems at home.

Since 1964 we have had the opportunity of seeing just what is the Treasury reaction to high unemployment and a weak pound. In 1976, with the level of unemployment at a record post-war level of one and a quarter million, the pound sank to unprecedentedly low levels against the United States dollar. The Labour Chancellor plunged into advocacy of public expenditure cuts and rigid monetarism. We can be sure that he had the whole-hearted backing of many senior Treasury men, and therefore Samuel Brittan's fear that a pre-war, pre-Keynes mentality held sway in the senior economic councils of the land was proved.

Various attempts were made to set Britain on a high growth path by expansionist policies. In particular, the most full-blooded of these was the attempt by the Conservative administration in 1972. This was defeated by the oil crisis of 1973. It is by no means certain that the failure of this attempt at spirited Keynesian economics proved that the route should not be tried again – but it set the scene for a monetarist revival under the new Labour Chancellor.

Chapter 7 deals with events from the oil crisis year of 1973 onwards; lack of commitment on the part of politicians to economic planning which they had accepted as part of the pre-election programme, and the drift of Labour politicians towards the Treasury mentality of the 1920s. All of which recalls Harold Macmillan's description of Labour ministers in 1931:

> But the real charge against the Labour Cabinet as a whole is not that they differed in principle with the Treasury view, but that they did not follow out the logical sequence of the principles which they had accepted. It was true that there were bolder spirits, such as Leo Amery or Keynes, who might, if they had been in charge, have followed a different course. But the Labour Ministers, whatever they may have protested later, cannot claim to have been anything except obedient devotees of the classical creed. In a word, they accepted the diagnosis but refused to apply the cure. [3]

The Treasury view to which ministers turned from 1976 onwards was, however, the pre-war, pre-Keynesian view of the world that was being revived by the monetarist school of economic thought. The pre-1976 Treasury advice was more benign, but not supported by active preparation to deal with a sterling crisis of major proportions. By the time Labour lost the crucial election of 1979, they had completed preparatory work for the fervid monetarists of the new administration. The new Conservative government, accepting the antique analysis of Britain's problems, had no hesitation in applying the antique cure. The opposition was in the embarrassing position of having to oppose a full-blooded application of the very monetary principles which they themselves had vocally supported. The old Treasury rules were being applied – although just how enthusiastic all the Treasury officials might be for them seems dubious.

From 1925 to 1980, manufacturing and industrial interests have been consistently sacrificed to abstract doctrine and, above all, the strength of the pound. And paradoxically, Labour administrations have proved just as willing as any Conservative administration to follow this path. The suspicion that officials discriminate carefully over what they are prepared to advise ministers of different political colours on which options really are available is confirmed anecdotally. Unfortunately, Whitehall's distance from the real world of industry is so enormous that the continuation of such political game-playing at industry's expense seems potentially indefinite. Under the present system, ministers can blame permanent officials for not applying policies, or not warning of impending crises, and officials can blame politicians for either not knowing what they want to do, or for not listening to reason. In a curious way, this arrangement is comfortable for both parties, but it is highly damaging for the effective application of policy. The cult of professional administrators who are not effectively accountable to anyone, and have very limited knowledge of the 'outside world', is very dangerous. The supreme skill of the senior civil servant today is in communicating with other senior civil servants and in keeping the existing machine running smoothly. The fact that it is running downhill at an apparently increasing pace is not a major concern. Lack of experience 'outside', stupidity and so on, are all charges that can be levelled against politicians, just as easily as at officials. But at least politicians are out in the open; we can hear their speeches, question them, and in the final analysis we can even see them thrown out of Parliament by the votes of their constituents.

No such remedy exists for the 'permanent' politicians. Chapter 8 suggests some ways in which the senior officials might be made more accountable, and more genuinely responsive, to the political decisions of their democratically elected masters.

At the national level, policies introduced in the name of 'sound money' and monetarism have been so extreme that a lurch back towards policies of growth rather than of decline may well occur within a few years. Those who have applied a doctrine of decline in the name of Adam Smith, should recall his words:

> It deserves to be remarked, perhaps, that it is in the progressive state, while the society is advancing to the further acquisition, rather than when it has acquired its full complement of riches, that the condition of the labouring poor, of the great body of the people, seems to be the happiest and the most comfortable. It is hard in the stationary, and miserable in the declining state. The progressive state is in reality the cheerful and the hearty state to all the different orders of the society. The stationary is dull; the declining, melancholy. [4]

## REFERENCES

1   Cole, G.D.H., *Practical Economics,* Pelican 1937, reprinted 1941, p.7
2   Brittan, Samuel, *The Treasury under the Tories 1951–64,* Pelican 1964, p.325
3   Macmillan, Harold, *Winds of Change, 1914–1939,* Macmillan 1966, p.269
4   Smith, Adam, *The Wealth of Nations,* 1776, reprinted Pelican 1976, ch. viii, p.184

# 2

# The Permanent Politicians

*The defects of bureaucracy are, indeed, well known. It is a form of Government which has been tried often enough in the world, and it is easy to show what, human nature being what it in the long run is, the defects of a bureaucracy must in the long run be.*

*Walter Bagehot,* The English Constitution, *1867*[1]

It was Bagehot in his work *The English Constitution*, published in 1867, who emphasized the importance of distinguishing between myth and reality in the British political system, the distinction between the 'dignified' and the 'efficient' parts of the established superstructure of government. In Bagehot's analysis, the dignified part of the constitutional apparatus was the monarch and the aristocracy. The efficient part was the House of Commons and the Cabinet. The dignified part had the important role of 'exciting and preserving the reverence of the population'. The efficient part ruled, in relative obscurity from the common man.

After the First World War, it could be argued, the Commons

9

joined the dignified part of the structure – and even Cabinet itself became ritualized as a rubber stamp on decisions made elsewhere. Bagehot described the Cabinet as a 'buckle' joining the legislature and the executive, a secret committee which kept no official minute. Today's parallel to such a secret co-ordinating committee could be the regular meeting of Permanent Secretaries to discuss govern-ment business, or possibly one of the shadowy official sub-commit-tees of senior civil servants meeting in obscurity and secrecy. But while Bagehot's secret committee had to face public exposure and questioning – which he thought would expose fools and foolishness – today's powerful bureaucrats face virtually no such test. Bagehot argued the dangers of bureaucracy as a form of government. He emphasized that bureaucracies were rigid in their responses to a changing world, and that they often lost sight of the underlying purpose of their existence.

> It is an inevitable defect, that bureaucrats will care more for routine than for results; – or, as Burke put it, 'that they will think the substance of business not to be much more important than the form of it'. . . Men so trained must come to think the routine of business not a means, but an end – to imagine the elaborate machinery of which they form a part, and from which they derive their dignity, to be a grand and achieved result, not a working and changeable instrument.[2]

It is as true today as it was in the nineteenth century that bureaucrats tend to lose sight of the wood for the trees. Careers are built upon intimate knowledge of the labyrinthine secret Whitehall world, and the more senior an official becomes, the more he will have invested his time in learning to manoeuvre within the existing structure. His opposition to change in structure and outlook will therefore increase as he is promoted. Similarly, as he grows older and more senior, he will hold more tenaciously to the doctrines that he learned as a young official. He will, furthermore, tend to favour for promotion those officials who are most like himself in culture and outlook and therefore least liable to cause the complex bureaucratic structure to be changed.

In Bagehot's view, the English system allowed ministry officials to have their inbred bureaucratic evils neutralized by respective ministers. The minister would bring in a fresh view of old problems, would question bureaucratic form, and have a wider and more common-sense view of problems. He could offer this from a wide experience outside government.

If left to itself, the office will become technical, self-absorbed, self-multiplying. It will be likely to overlook the end in the means; – it will fail from narrowness of mind; – it will be eager to be seeming to do; it will be idle in real doing. An extrinsic chief is the fit corrector of such errors. He can say to the permanent chief, skilled in the forms and pompous with the memories of his office, 'Will you, Sir, explain to me how this regulation conduces to the end in view?[3]

Bagehot emphasized the importance of freshening up the bureaucracies for a rapidly changing economy. For a stagnant society, he felt that a really well-designed bureaucracy might be adequate. In the twentieth century, his view that the British system would continue to force the ever-growing bureaucracies to adjust to reality seems to have foundered. Traditional bureaucratic doctrines have frequently proved stronger than many politicians of the greatest individuality, vision and strength, not because the bureaucrats really won arguments, presented special insights, or employed manoeuvres to win over ministers to their views. By controlling access to ministers, and by presenting a uniform front, their doctrines have often appeared to be universally true and accepted by all sensible men.

One particular economic doctrine that dominated all other cares and objectives at the Treasury in the period 1924 to 1938 was the return to the Gold Standard. This was held to be a touchstone of all economic virtue and success. Therefore much more effort was focused on persuading ministers of the need to return to the Gold Standard than to any other economic or financial goal. And yet the return to gold in 1925 did not yield any obvious beneficial results, and was in any event unstable (Chapter 4). The instability of a world system based on the virtues of balanced budgets and the international Gold Standard was well illustrated by events following 1929. Nevertheless, officials kept on hankering for yet another return in the 1930s while other problems multiplied. Despite growing international dangers, the Treasury was still providing arguments against greater rearmament expenditure in 1937 and 1938, and thus supporting Chamberlain's view that 'sound finance' was a better defence than military hardware. Economic management in the 1920s and 1930s was the dismal failure that could be expected of a most rigid application of doctrines of balanced budgets and sound finance. A clearer example of what Bagehot called 'confusion of the ends with the means' occurred in the post-war period, when planning was given form though little substance. It must be admitted that officials at these various points in time could always point to people outside the Whitehall machinery who supported their view. In the 1920s, many people did support the Gold Standard. Businessmen did expect budgets to be rigidly balanced. Similarly, in the 1940s, there was great suspicion in the business community of control and planning. Even the Labour Cabinet shied away from very extensive planning of the economy, virtually from the first few Cabinet meetings after their election in 1945. Therefore, it would be wrong to believe that the bureaucracy hatched its own policy in isolation.

The social nature and 'corporate view' of the Whitehall bureaucrat is clearly important in understanding his bias against positive policies, and what he would be likely to recommend in a crisis. His outlook also explains his predilection for fundamentally negative behaviour, and therefore for negative policies. The present inadequacy of government structure to generate or apply positive economic policies to counter Britain's dangerous course of decline is therefore nothing new

Taking Bagehot's point on the need to 'ventilate' the executive, a very important part of any future regeneration of Britain's industrial and economic resources must be played by the greater professionalism and enhanced role of our politicians. But no matter how good our politicians are, they will make little progress unless the government departments have sufficient quality and morale to tackle the job in hand. Just as Jean Monnet (the instigator of the first European Community and post-war industrial planning in France) admired the success of the French bureaucracy in maintaining the state of affairs entrusted to it (see page 80), we must marvel at the way in which the British bureaucrat has kept the British machinery of economic decision-making as near unchanged as possible over the past fifty years. It is no doubt true in the short run that a slow-growing economy is easier to handle than a fast-growing one. Just as Monnet regarded the French Civil Service of 1945 as unsuitable for instituting a national plan of modernization, the British experience has shown that the British mandarin has, in general, lacked the spirit of enterprise which Monnet felt was necessary for such an undertaking. Furthermore, Monnet learned from the mistakes he believed were inherent in the first British attempts at post-war planning under Cripps, whereas in Britain, no one seems to have attempted to learn either from mistakes in France, or from success. Monnet noted that it might be necessary to plan to transform the French establishment. If we were to consider a massive change in direction of policies in Britain, we should also consider just how deeply embedded is our own establishment, particularly the permanent politicians of Whitehall.

Schoolchildren are taught that policies are determined by Cabinet, and executed by officials. To quote from a GCE 'O' level textbook:

> The policy decided upon by the Cabinet is put into effect by the various departments of State. Thus it is the particular department which is responsible for:
> (a) drawing up the necessary legislation and piloting it through Parliament;
> (b) setting up the organisation to implement that legislation;
> (c) carrying out the day-to-day tasks imposed by previous legislation.
> . . . The division of departments according to function is a convenient form of organisation. The danger, however is that a department may tend to regard itself as a watertight compartment whereas, in fact its work overlaps with others. Means must therefore be found of achieving co-ordination. Much co-ordination is of an informal nature. Those who work in the departments form a unified civil service and follow common methods. This facilitates the interchange of ideas and makes it easier for them to pull together. An official can easily contact his opposite number in another department by telephone. 'If he's awkward,' one has said, 'I invite him round for a cup of tea. If he's particularly awkward, I give him a piece of cake.'[4]

In this rather cosy view of the Constitution, the 'O' level candidate is introduced to the idea that the permanent civil servant may actually institute policy, although:

> As civil servants, they are politically neutral. Their tasks are:
> (1) to advise the minister on proposed policy, providing

information and suggesting (even to the point of exaggerating) administrative difficulties, not with the object of being obstructive, but in order to ensure that the policy is workable;

(2) to suggest policy;

(3) to administer policies decided upon . . .[5]

It is also interesting that this modern work, initiating the next generation to the British political process, emphasizes the extent to which the Treasury is the linchpin of the administration.

Sir Warren Fisher's evidence to the 1929 Royal Commission on the Civil Service was for many years regarded as the definitive statement on the issue of the origin of policy.

Determination of policy is the function of ministers, and once a policy is determined it is the unquestioned and unquestionable business of the civil servant to strive to carry out that policy with precisely the same good will whether he agrees with it or not. That is axiomatic and will never be in dispute. At the same time it is the traditional duty of civil servants, while decisions are being formulated, to make available to their political chiefs all the information and experience at their disposal, and to do this without fear or favour, irrespective of whether the advice thus tendered may accord or not with the minister's initial view.[6]

This has a distinctly different flavour from the task of 'suggesting policy', and seems odd when considering the actual economic advice being offered to Chancellors during the inter-war period. Indeed the clinical division of role defined by Warren Fisher squares uneasily with his own advice to a Prime Minister about suitable political appointments (see page 17). Naturally, few of those present at the 1929 Commission would have had the opportunity of going through the records of then contemporary Treasury advice to Chancellors, as we have today. For example, knowledge of the way in which Germany financed rearmament was available to Treasury officials in 1935 through to 1938, yet they resolutely argued the case of financial stringency on first (and erroneous) principles. We have noted elsewhere (page 69), in memoranda sent to Warren Fisher, how they had expected Germany to suffer a financial collapse as a result of rearmament. It can be assumed that if those prognostications had had verification in fact, they would have been brought up in the arguments over rearmament later on.

In Sir Ivor Jennings's authoritative study of the workings of British government, it was at least accepted that the permanent official would have strong views on policy, although it was not suggested that he would himself initiate policy:

> It is inevitable that he should develop and give expression to views of his own and that the department as a whole should adopt and seek to give effect to principles of action which arise out of the common experience of its senior members. It would be difficult to give specific examples because any such principles would not be expressed in writing; they would be the sum of the 'inarticulate major premises' of the officials concerned, and would be imperfectly known to the officials themselves. They would appear as the basis of minutes and memoranda and could be traced only by a careful comparison of the action recommended and taken with the conditions in which the recommendations were made. Such examples as may be cited are mere allegations, insusceptible of proof.

> It was assumed before the depression of 1929–33 that the Treasury was dominated by the principles of 'Gladstonian finance', which attributed the highest virtue to balancing the Budget and would have scorned such a policy as President Franklin D. Roosevelt's 'New Deal'. It was assumed, too, that the Treasury and even more the Board of Trade (because it was concerned primarily with the encouragement of exports) was until 1932 (at least) convinced of the validity of the free trade doctrine. It was alleged that the Foreign Office under Sir Robert Vansittart was Germanophobe and Francophile. . . Nevertheless, the tradition is firm that when the Government changes the policy, the departmental policy must change. . . while the 'spoils system' is not in operation, it is not always possible for ministers to continue to work with senior civil servants who have strong views on policy.[7]

References in Chapters 4 and 5 will indicate that the Treasury's thinking on budgetary matters *was* rigidly 'Gladstonian', both before and after the depression, with far-reaching implications. Similarly, the thinking of the Treasury seems to have been 'free trade' over the same period despite massive improvement in

15

prosperity after the implementation of protectionist tariffs. As has been said before in the context of the departure from the Gold Standard in 1931, the adoption of alternative policies represented the victory of economic forces over doctrine, not the willingness of civil servants to follow new government policies.

At least in more modern textbooks, it is becoming accepted that the administrative machine cannot really be neutral, and that greater openness of government will be needed to offset the kinds of bias which the Civil Service machine may exhibit in secrecy.

Realization of the significance of Civil Service power has been growing steadily:

> Here again there has been considerable exaggeration on the part of some critics, particularly those who talk in terms of the replacement of ministerial responsibility by civil service dictatorship. Such dictatorship is a figment of the imagination; reality is to be found in the concoction of policy in semi-secret by a triad of Ministers, civil servants and pressure-group representatives, with Parliament hovering critically and vocally in the background, sometimes able to influence policy even in a radical way, at others being forced to accept a series of *faits accomplis*. More serious critics demand not that the triad should be broken up (which would be undesirable as well as impossible) but that its operation should be brought more out into the open and exposed more thoroughly to the light of public and parliamentary criticism. This demand, once condemned as extreme, seems well on the way to becoming current doctrine. [8]

It is not clear whether all civil servants heartily support a triad which would include ministers. Some prominent ex-civil servants have become, of late, much more free in their criticisms of ministerial power. Baroness Sharp, Permanent Secretary at the Ministry of Housing and Local Government between 1955 and 1966, served as chief civil servant beneath some half dozen ministers from both the Labour Party and the Conservative Party. She emerged in Richard Crossman's diaries as a formidable figure, and since retirement became something of a front runner in the civil servants' counter campaign against ministers. She commented in a radio programme in May 1975 on the inadequacy which she perceived in ministerial government:

> What we really come back to is the heart of government,

which is Ministers – potential Ministers. Now don't we really need much more of presidential or Prime Ministerial style of government, to grapple with the immense complication and confusion of government now? In other words it'll need far stronger leadership, because as you're saying, it's no good getting a bunch of people, twenty or whatever it is, all coming here with policies worked out on this, that and the other, or in fact there's got to be a central strategy for government, conditioned by economic possibilities which really does need leaders' determination and the laying down of the lines for all concerned. [9]

It is well worth pondering the implications of these mysterious phrases. Baroness Sharp seems to be saying that government by a committee of politicians – the Cabinet – is inadequate, since no 'central strategy' emerges. She believes that we need more 'presidential' government – direction by one man or woman – so that the 'immense complication' of government could be managed. But of course, this 'immense complication' could not be handled by one person. A committee would be needed, with individuals specializing in various fields of government. She is suggesting that politicians are not adequate for this job, since they come to Cabinet with 'policies worked out on this, that and the other' which, horror of horrors, might not be conditioned by 'economic possibilities'. Obviously, a committee of senior civil servants should decide in advance what the 'economic possibilities' are, and if the top policy-making committee also consisted of senior civil servants, with one politician in the chair, no one would waste time arguing about the 'possibilities', because no one would disagree with the view set out by the Treasury.

Strong feelings amongst senior civil servants about the way in which ministers ought to fit into the scheme of things have existed for a long time. On occasion, this concern has extended to giving advice to the Prime Minister himself about the 'right man' for a certain ministerial job. In 1936, Sir Maurice Hankey, Secretary to the Cabinet, wrote to Warren Fisher, the head of the Treasury: 'After today's debate I am afraid we have got to make some concession for a Minister of Defence. What I want is something that will work and not upset the psychology of the whole machine.'

Warren Fisher wrote to Chamberlain: 'The Minister should be a disinterested type of man, with no axe to grind or desire to make a

17

place for himself.' The civil servant head of the Treasury went on to recommend Lord Halifax as the most suitable man.[10] It is interesting to note that Lord Halifax became a leading 'appeaser' in the foreign policy debates of the late 1930s.

This aspect of civil servant influence is rarely, if ever, mentioned in textbooks on constitutional theory. It does offer the intriguing possibility that Prime Ministers are themselves occasionally given or perhaps seek advice from the permanent civil servants concerning the appointments to Cabinet itself. Nevertheless, any Prime Minister has also to consider the reception any ministerial appointment would receive from his parliamentary party, at least as weightily as the Civil Service reception. The importance ratio would depend upon the Prime Minister. It would nevertheless be stretching the imagination very far indeed to believe that the most senior civil servants do not get involved in what are clearly political, rather than technical, issues relating to ministers' activities. The example above shows a clear expectation upon Warren Fisher's part that his view on a new ministerial appointment would be taken seriously, and that it was within his scope, as Permanent Secretary at the Treasury, to recommend a specific name for appointment at the new ministry.

In fact, his own relationship with Neville Chamberlain was close, as the following letter, dated 1 June 1936, indicates:

> Neville Dear – I did enjoy getting a little note from you – it gives such a cosy feeling. Bless you. That's a truly delightful paper about Bullock, isn't it? But there's no escape from the consequences. With fond love, Warren.[11]

At such a level of intimacy with his political 'master', direct political advice may have seemed a natural part of his function.

Strong personalities among senior civil servants today are not averse to passing judgements on the quality and role of ministers. Lord Armstrong, head of the Civil Service from 1968 to 1974, in answering criticism that civil servants attempted to manipulate ministers, commented in 1977:

> My experience has been much more of a Minister not leaving himself time to consider a decision because of his own failure to deal with a report he has been given until the last minute. Richard Crossman's room used to be full of undecided planning

cases. The last thing he wanted to do was incur the odium of taking a decision. Evelyn Sharp [Crossman's Permanent Secretary] had to get him by the scruff of the neck and force him to go through them. He hated it. [12]

Although it is clear from Baroness Sharp's comments quoted above that there is some irritation among civil servants recently with Cabinet government, as opposed to Prime Ministerial government, Lord Armstrong attempted in this interview to reassert the Cabinet principle while sharply criticizing one Cabinet minister:

This problem led to considerable difficulties when Wedgie Benn was on the rampage at the Department of Industry. He was a member of the Cabinet, but pulling in a direction that the Government didn't like. That was a very unhappy time for civil servants in his department. [13]

Lord Armstrong did not explain that Tony Benn was attempting to implement Labour Party policy, as embodied in various documents accepted by Labour Party Conference. Since Cabinet had not instructed Tony Benn to abstain from the actions which his civil servants were resisting, it is rather difficult to understand what Lord Armstrong meant at this point by 'Government'. Plausibly, he meant the Prime Minister himself, since we know that in the summer of 1974 Harold Wilson attempted a rewrite of the major Department of Industry White Paper drafted by Eric Heffer and Tony Benn.

Lord Armstrong introduced a further and much more startling constitutional statement in the same interview:

In my experience, the present system of allowing Ministers to bring in political assistants works perfectly well, though there may be cases of civil servants who resent it.

But it's quite another thing to go to the full length that Sedgemore* wants, akin to the United States where the entire top layer in a department are political appointees, and a career civil servant can rarely expect to get to the policy-making layer. [14]

Thus in Lord Armstrong's view, the 'top layer' permanent civil

---

*Brian Sedgemore – Labour MP for Luton, 1974–79, author and former civil servant.

servants in any department are not just policy advisers and executors, but they are policy makers – they are, and in his view should
be, making policy.

Belief that the role of the senior civil servant has increased
dramatically in importance over the past few decades is held with
conviction across the political spectrum. Michael Wolff, who was
an appointee of Edward Heath to the Prime Minister's office in
1970, wrote in *The Times* in 1976 that the Civil Service had managed
to adapt well to modern conditions, despite its antiquated structure:

> The result, however, is a recognisable shift of power away
> from the elected politician to the bureaucracy. It would be
> wrong to close one's eyes to the fact that, in Sir Eric Roll's
> words, 'the tradition that ministers take the political decisions
> and civil servants carry them out has long been overtaken by
> reality'. It is no secret that over the past decade or two the civil
> servants at the Treasury have taken a positive, if not actually
> aggressive policy line over pay and price restraints and sterling
> devaluation…Mr John Peyton's experience is that a minister
> cannot be sure that something will be done unless it is some-
> thing the civil servants want. 'They are unresponsive to the
> temporary tenant. A new minister finds himself dazzled by the
> grand language of the Civil Service boss words.' [15]

Thus, despite the general textbook view that civil servants advise
on and execute policy, the generally accepted fact is that they have
acquired enough power to consider themselves as policy-makers
into the bargain. The minister remains as a shield for the top layer
of civil servants, and may, against the odds, make some policy
himself. But if the civil servants suspect that the minister may be
moved within a year or so, we have John Peyton's view that the civil
servants will be 'unresponsive to the temporary tenant'. Lord
Crowther-Hunt reached similar conclusions after his many years of
studying and analysing the government machinery. In a newspaper
article published in 1977 he made three powerful points: firstly,
that Civil Service power vis à vis ministers has greatly increased this
century. Secondly, that the Civil Service has quickly absorbed rival
power centres set up inside Whitehall by governments anxious to
offset the influence of the bureaucracy. And finally, that 'while this
general expansion of bureaucratic power has been taking place,
successive governments have manifestly failed to deal successfully
with the nation's affairs. Indeed, were it not for the bonanza from

North Sea oil our economic and social problems would now be virtually insoluble.' [16]

A few years on, we can now conclude that the economic malaise has become so bad that, even with North Sea oil, our problems are quite insoluble by the old methods. But this situation is the product of the old approaches to economic management – deflation under Jenkins and Healey to deal with a balance of payments problem, followed by the application of primitive pre-war monetarism under Healey and Howe. Only under Barber was a major attempt made to break out of the vicious circle of stagnation and industrial decline. Significantly, Barber was one of the few recent Chancellors to take both City opinion and Treasury advice with a substantial pinch of salt.

The measure of disdain which many senior civil servants have for ministers is often translated into active manipulation. Fred Hirsch, a former International Monetary Fund official who went on to become Professor of International Studies at the University of Warwick, quoted in a newspaper article four examples of what he considered to be the arrogation of ministerial power by the Civil Service in the economic sphere. The three which were from his own first-hand experience are as follows. In July 1975, a sudden fall in sterling precipitated the Labour government into the first phase of their series of incomes policy stages which involved substantial falls in real take home pay for the average wage earner. Hirsch wrote:

> The Treasury's at least passive encouragement of the fall in sterling was obvious to most close observers at the time. A week or two later, a high Treasury official encapsuled the episode to me in the following terse comment: 'We organised a bear raid on sterling in an attempted coup d'état against trade union government; unfortunately we failed.' Tongue nicely in cheek, but not too far. [17]

It should be explained that, as was revealed by Harold Wilson's Press Secretary at that time, the Treasury had hoped for a compulsory incomes policy, with penal sanctions against trade unions. The Treasury began to commend a compulsory pay policy to the Chancellor at the end of 1974, coincidentally just after ministerial approval had been obtained for a large increase in senior civil servants' pay.

Professor Hirsch also noted the way that the Bank of England can work with the Treasury to obtain either favourable or less favourable terms for IMF loans to British governments. The manner in which a general impression of Britain's problems is conveyed to the IMF mission is very much in the hands of officials. In 1969, the IMF mission was urged by officials at the Bank of England to meet City representatives. Hirsch recalled:

> One by one the City bankers and financiers reeled off their complaints against the Labour Government and its policy, to the growing embarrassment of the IMF mission chief, David Finch. 'Gentlemen,' he eventually riposted, 'In our assessment the authorities have now taken rather extensive corrective measures in a tricky situation: what specifically do you want the Chancellor to do in addition?' From across the table came a one word answer: 'Resign.' In the ensuing silence the banker realised his gaffe. But since the IMF, like any other leading banker, will always prefer to err on the side of the over-tough conditions that ensure its own scheduled repayment, domestic pressures of this kind undoubtedly help to stiffen the eventual loan terms. [18]

In 1969, contrary to IMF expectations, British officials failed to press for a larger increase in the British 'quota' – Britain's margin of credit afforded by the IMF. From his own inside knowledge of the IMF at the time, Hirsch knew that the IMF management believed that the UK could not really be denied a larger increase than that initially held out in negotiation. British officials would have had the same inside knowledge – but they accepted the initial IMF offer.

> The legitimate complaint against the Treasury establishment is that it has failed in its own purpose. In manipulating information and tailoring advice to the anticipated response, the Treasury has not found any royal road to success. Of course, the Treasury could never achieve this by itself. Its failing has been its compulsive instinct, born perhaps equally of arrogance and of defensiveness, to keep the structure of policy formulation in its own hands. [19]

The picture that emerges of the permanent politicians is therefore one of strong-minded individuals who are quite uninhibited in building up independent views on policy, and in developing attitudes that are at times sharply critical of the existing political structure. They have been known to develop considerable intimacy with their political masters, and these days feel free to express degrees of contempt for politicians alive and dead.

The examples quoted above were criticisms by ex-civil servants and ex-ministers. They nevertheless illustrate quite clearly that the senior civil servant regards himself or herself as being in a class apart from the politician, who is expected, under our democratic process, to take the blame or glory for government policies. The quality of advice emanating from the claustrophobic corridors of the Treasury – which we may expect from Bagehot's precepts to be dubious – is discussed later in the book. The nature of this 'class apart' is the topic for consideration in the next chapter.

# REFERENCES

1 Bagehot, Walter, *The English Constitution*, reprinted Fontana 1963, p.195
2 ibid.
3 Bagehot, op. cit., p.199
4 Harvey, J., *How Britain is Governed*, Macmillan 1970, pp.143-45
5 Harvey, op. cit., pp.148–49
6 Royal Commission on the Civil Service, 1929, Minutes of Evidence, p.1268
7 Jennings, Sir Ivor, *Cabinet Government*, 2nd ed., Cambridge University Press 1951, pp.116–18
8 Hanson, A. H. and Walles, M., *Governing Britain*, Fontana 1975, p.149
9 Baroness Sharp, speaking on BBC Radio 4, 'A Word in Edgeways', 22 May 1975
10 Gilbert, Martin, *Winston S. Churchill*, vol. 5, Heinemann 1976, pp.705–707
11 NC 7/11/29/20 quoted in Peden, G. C., *British Rearmament and the Treasury*, Scottish Academic Press 1979, p.56
12 *Observer*, 18 September 1977 – interview with Laurence Marks
13 ibid.
14 ibid.
15 *The Times*, 27 May 1976
16 *Guardian*, 20 May 1977

17 *Guardian*, 18 February 1977
18 ibid.
19 ibid.

# 3

# The Class Apart – Mandarin Society

*The civil service in Britain today is an élite arrogating to itself political power in a manner which betokens trouble for democracy... The majority of top administrative civil servants (i.e. those who advise ministers on policy) come from a narrow social class, went to public schools and to Oxford or Cambridge and obtained a good degree in an arts subject... The conventional wisdom (which I have never understood) holds that these are the best people to govern and administer the country.*
Brian Sedgemore, The Secret Constitution, *1980*[1]

The aspirations of bureaucrats for power are understandable enough. Their self-confidence in exercising it, the objectives which they aim at, and what they identify as problems to be solved are all questions which can be much better answered if we understand the social as well as the constitutional position of today's civil servant.

A key aspect of the social status is their highly protected job position. Once a civil servant has reached the higher levels of the policy-making layer, he is automatically cushioned from the kind of career and job threats that face his contemporaries in business or in other professions. For, besides security, there is the enormous protection of secrecy. No journalist is ever likely to be able to read advice or instructions given to ministers during the career lifetime of the advisers. And ministers are not able to check what sort of advice has been given to their predecessors by the same senior men, if they are part of a new government. No other profession is able to ensure that its tracks are so well covered by the statute book itself.

With such advantages, it was once assumed that a compensating factor to ensure social equity was reduced financial rewards for public administrators. Now advice on the implementation of the top salary review board is given to ministers by top civil servants. In 1974, senior ministers were advised that failure to implement the recommended increase of around 29% would lead to serious damage to the morale of top civil servants. Perhaps the same kind of advice was given over the implementation of inflation proof pensions. It is interesting to note that the partial approval of these increases was agreed by Cabinet members shortly before the first documents went to the Chancellor recommending a tough pay policy.

As has been observed by Roger Berthoud:

It is perhaps more important that we should question the British scale of values, which (as the Boyle Report pointed out) gives our senior Civil servants, judges and generals, broadly the same salaries as their EEC equivalents (rather higher in many instances), while managerial salaries are roughly half those in north-west Europe, as any large company knows. This was the main point of Shell's memorandum to the Diamond Commission, implicitly suggesting that Civil Service salaries should revert to the market concept of 'enough to attract and retain'.[2]

The Boyle Report of December 1974 gave the following comparable figures for the salaries of Permanent Secretaries in various countries in Northern Europe on the basis of data available at that time:

Table 1: *Salaries and compensation for Permanent Secretaries and approximate equivalents in Civil Services of European countries, September 1973*[3]

|  | Basic salary | Gross salary before tax | Title |
|---|---|---|---|
| UK | £16,000 | £15,900 | Permanent Secretary |
| Belgium | £9,000 | £9,791 | Secrétaire Général |
| Italy | £8,360 | £9,025 | State General Accountant, Prefect |
| Netherlands | £12,360 | £12,335 | Secretary General |
| France | £8,541 | £9,565 | Directeur Général, E. |
| W. Germany | £12,328 | £14,564 | Direktor des Bundesrates |

(Various problems of comparability are explained in the source.)

Considering the divergence between these countries in terms of average wages and National Income per capita, these figures are little short of astonishing. For comparison, figures quoted by the Organization for Economic Cooperation and Development for Gross Domestic Income in 1974 allow per capita figures of national output to be calculated for 1974:

Table 2: *Gross Domestic Product at 1974 prices and exchange rates*[4]

|  | Billions of dollars | Population, millions | GDP per head, dollars |
|---|---|---|---|
| UK | 186.8 | 56.0 | 3336 |
| Belgium | 52.9 | 9.8 | 5398 |
| Italy | 149.0 | 55.4 | 2690 |
| Holland | 70.1 | 13.5 | 5193 |
| France | 274.0 | 52.6 | 5209 |
| W.Germany | 385.7 | 62.1 | 6211 |

Thus, although in 1973 the UK was evidently the second poorest country among those represented, the pay for the top civil servant in Britain was apparently well ahead of the rest. West Germany with a per capita Gross Domestic Product 86% higher than Britain's in 1974, actually paid its top civil servants 23% less at the end of the preceding year.

Given the problems of comparability, small divergences of salary and relative salary should not be taken as very significant. What is important is that the divergences for senior civil servant pay indicated in the Boyle Report were gross, and in inverse relationship to the economic state of the nations examined. On the other hand, divergences in pay for industrial executives were clearly more in line with the relative economic strength of the countries. The indications are that this type of divergence between the relative position of the British industrial executive and his contemporary in the higher Civil Service has continued, while the security of the business executive has markedly declined.

Some defence for the superior pay position of senior British civil servants might be offered if there were any evidence that major increases in Civil Service productivity at the higher level had taken place. If their numbers had sharply declined over the past few years, for instance, we might believe that whatever it is they may do, they do it more efficiently than before. However, as Britain's industry has declined, the number of senior civil servants has augmented.

From 1965 to 1980, the number of Permanent Secretaries in the Home Civil Service rose from thirty-seven to forty-one – their salaries from £8,060 to £27,768 per annum. Business was obviously better for Deputy Secretaries who increased in numbers from ninety-two to 157, and in salary (median for the grade) from £5,800 to £22,500. Under Secretaries really proved to be in the boom sector, however, increasing numbers by a magnificent 82% from 324 to 590.[5] Meanwhile, employment in Great Britain's manufacturing sector fell by more than 20%. Did productivity in the public sector increase with the added top brass? Certainly not from the point of view of cutting down the allocation of people to the public sector whilst increasing output, since the administrative machine's employment itself rose by 20% or so. But who is to say what the increase in output was?

The bias towards the very pinnacle of Britain's social élite is quite clear. In 1973, as an external candidate, a man's chance of selection was 29% if he came from Oxford or Cambridge, falling to 6% if he came from any other university. For women in 1973, a non-Oxbridge candidate stood only a 9% chance of appointment, as an external applicant. An Oxbridge candidate stood a 43% chance, over four times as high.

The argument put forward by the Commissioners to support the contention that there is no bias towards Oxford and Cambridge applicants is that the proportion of 'highest quality' schoolchildren going to Oxford and Cambridge is itself disproportionate, so this would be reflected in Civil Service entrants to the 'fast stream', the highest administrative posts. Questioned before the House of Commons Expenditure Committee, the Civil Service Commissioners – who are the officials charged with recruitment for the higher levels in the service –responded as follows:

Q.    If you remember, Lord Franks when he investigated Oxford, pointed out that their intake was biased. . . As I said, we are not investigating that. What we are investigating is whether there is any bias between the output of Oxbridge – it might be other universities – and your intake. That is what we want to determine at some stage, although I do not think it can be determined this afternoon.

A.    May I add one important fact? It is a fact which was quoted in the Davies Committee's report, which indicates that Oxford and Cambridge attract nearly one third of the most able children judged by their performance at advanced level, although in fact the two universities between them take only one tenth of the university places.[6]

Statistically, the argument implied by the Commissioners is fallacious. If one accepts the hypothesis that one-third of the most able students form part of the Oxbridge throughput, then necessarily, two-thirds of the most able students *do not* go to Oxbridge. Furthermore, if the tendency of the most able students to apply for administrative trainee entrance to the Civil Service is the same in both Oxbridge and other universities, the proportion of acceptances to the Civil Service should be one-third Oxbridge, and two-thirds non-Oxbridge. Over the years 1971–75 it can be seen that Oxbridge has achieved an average success rate of 58% of the men, and even with a much smaller proportion of women Oxbridge applicants, 37% of the women. This bias is very highly improbable as a result of chance.

No doubt the Commissioners could further argue that for some reason or other, there is a systematic tendency for the bright students who do not go to Oxford or Cambridge not to apply for

**Table 3:** *Administrative trainee posts in the Civil Service, external graduate applicants and appointees*[7]

*MEN*

|  | 1971 | 1972 | 1973 | 1974 | 1975 |
|---|---|---|---|---|---|
| Proportion of applicants from Oxford and Cambridge | 25.9% | 27.1% | 27.2% | 27.7% | 25.6% |
| Applicant records examined | 844 | 1154 | 1142 | 923 | 1204 |
| Proportion of appointees from Oxford and Cambridge | 57.9% | 53.8% | 56.6% | 61.6% | 61.5% |
| Total number of appointee records examined | 83 | 91 | 138 | 130 | 143 |

*WOMEN*

|  | 1971 | 1972 | 1973 | 1974 | 1975 |
|---|---|---|---|---|---|
| Proportion of applicants from Oxford and Cambridge | 12.7% | 13.5% | 11.1% | 11.3% | 13.0% |
| Applicant records examined | 409 | 637 | 587 | 583 | 746 |
| Proportion of appointees from Oxford and Cambridge | 44.2% | 23.3% | 37.8% | 29.0% | 51.9% |
| Total number of appointee records examined | 43 | 43 | 74 | 62 | 52 |

Table 4: *Administrative trainees, appointments and applications from 'public' and fee-paying schools (from outside the Civil Service)*[8]

## MEN

| External | 1971 | 1972 | 1973 | 1974 | 1975 |
|---|---|---|---|---|---|
| Applicants: proportion from direct grant, public and other fee-paying schools | 36.8% | 37.0% | 31.2% | 28.6% | 33.7% |
| Appointees: proportion of successes from above | 50.6% | 50.0% | 38.8% | 61.7% | 45.7% |
| Number of applicants from outside the Civil Service (records investigated) | 83 | 92 | 103 | 47 | 140 |

entry to the fast promotion stream of the Civil Service. This in itself would be a significant and grave issue for the Commissioners to attend to. They would have to discover why the bright non-Oxbridge students did not bother to apply to the Civil Service in the same proportion as their Oxbridge counterparts. Furthermore, as a matter of national interest, the Commissioners would presumably feel duty bound to make attempts to rectify the situation. The very fact that the Commissioners showed themselves quite content with the status quo during their evidence to the House of Commons inquiry illustrated that they either did not recognize or accept that there was any bias in their method of selection. Yet the statistical point made above demonstrates conclusively that the bias shown in the Commissioners' own figures can hardly be the product of chance, but the product of a persistent, unrelenting preference in the selection system towards the Oxbridge product.

31

A further interesting point from the Commissioners' evidence to the committee, was the preponderance of arts and humanities graduates amongst appointments of administrative trainees. In 1975, only 17% of appointees among men applying from outside the Civil Service had undertaken natural science or applied science degree courses. Among women, the percentage was 21% from external appointees. It is quite true that the proportion of applicants from outside the Civil Service with science or applied science backgrounds was very similar to those proportions accepted. But is it safe to assume that the proportions with the appropriate administrative abilities among science and engineering faculties are as low as would be implied by these figures? If it is true then it is a serious reflection upon the type of bias in our educational selection for engineers and scientists away from those with administrative and communicative skills. It also might indicate that those particular disciplines prevent individuals from acquiring the necessary administrative skills, like the ability to communicate clearly and to grasp arguments quickly. Alternatively, it might well reflect the knowledge of many science and engineering students that the Civil Service Commissioners are generally looking for 'good all rounders' from Oxbridge, so that it would be a waste of time even for the most able science and engineering students to bother applying.

Whatever underlies this particular aspect of the selectivity of the Civil Service in its appointments for the fast-promotion stream it is worrying that the great majority of future senior civil servants begin their careers poorly equipped to understand many technical aspects of industry, medicine, and the environment, as well as defence and energy. Curiously enough, the Civil Service actually appears to be proud of its 'talented amateur' approach to most problems. An interesting example of this attitude was given in comments made by Lord Armstrong, formerly head of the Home Civil Service, in the context of the disturbing revelations of the Tribunal into the 'V & G' affair. The Vehicle and General insurance company collapsed in circumstances which indicated inadequate performance on the part of certain civil servants concerned.

The V & G Tribunal muddied the waters still further by advancing the novel concept that merely by occupying senior posts, civil servants 'hold themselves out as persons exercising special skill in that particular field'.

'That did not make any sense at all to civil servants,' recalls

Lord Armstrong, who, as Head of the Home Civil Service in 1972, bore the brunt of the FDA's* complaints about the Tribunal's findings.

'We didn't think that we held ourselves out as competent. We were just appointed because other people thought we were. We might have had private doubts about it.'[9]

The cult of the amateur also plays its part in the Treasury. This has particularly serious implications when the Treasury has to deal with issues specifically covered by the activities of the Bank of England, such as dealings related to the strength of sterling and 'foreign confidence', since by contrast the Bank of England places emphasis on genuine expertise in financial matters.

To quote from Henry Roseveare's meticulous history of the Treasury:

> The Bank. . . usually drew all the strength it needed by traditional top-level appointments from the City-bred *élite*, or – more rarely and less traditionally – from its own trained executives. Both were narrow sources of ability and, as far as leadership is concerned, 1946 saw no abrupt break with Montagu Norman's legacy.[10]

It might be noted in passing that Montagu Norman, who was Governor of the Bank of England from 1922 to 1944, played a very significant role in the return to the Gold Standard, which had dire consequences for British industry (see Chapter 4). Furthermore, according to Fred Hirsch, documents released in the US reveal that he was most significant in preventing funds being made available to support the pound under the Labour government in 1931.[11]

The post-war Labour government made no move to protect itself from these unfriendly influences: '. . . Lord Cobbold [Governor from 1949 to 1961] was a Norman protégé, and the post-war Bank continued to have the services of such veterans of the 1930s as H.A. Siepman and Sir Otto Niemeyer'.[12] Certainly the Bank of England seemed to have gone out of its way to equip itself with 1930 vintage veterans, if not heroes. The Treasury, even if it wished to redress the balance with the Bank, never seems to have been suitably

---

* The First Division Association (FDA) is the trade union for senior civil servants.

prepared. Speaking to the Radcliffe Committee in 1958, Lord Bridges, a former long-serving Treasury mandarin, said of the Bank:

> The high officials of the Bank of England have long and intense training and experience in their particular field. They are specialists who have risen to the top through their skill and experience. . . On the other hand, officers of the Treasury are laymen in the sense that most of them do not spend much of their lives in becoming experts in any particular subject.[13]

And, naturally enough, as Roseveare commented:

> There was no question of the Treasury telling the Bank how to run its affairs, nor was there any question of the Bank becoming another department of the Treasury. Communications between them tended to pass at a high and privileged level, an aloof relationship which both sides liked to rationalise as one between banker and customer.[14]

This relationship between the Treasury and the Bank of England was certainly intact in the period 1974-76. Speeches and indications in the late 1970s show clearly that it exists up to the present day.

The issues of overwhelming importance, such as whether a run on the pound might be serious or not, whether it required a massive loan or stringent pay policy as a response, would therefore invariably find the Treasury obliged to accept the version of events as put to them by the Bank of England – because the Treasury would always lack the necessary expertise to cross-check the view put to them by the Bank. Only Chancellors or ministers who themselves had first hand knowledge of or good contacts in the City, might be able to resist the 'offers that could not be refused'.

It is all too easy to understand how small a step it is for senior men in the Treasury to 'swim with' advice or demands from the Bank of England rather than to take an independent line. In fact it could be argued that it is logical for officials to take advantage of the 'uncontrollable' forces of international finance to obtain objectives which would not be possible with a cool and calm group of ministers in Cabinet. The post-war Treasury has for long had a preference for pay policies as important instruments of control. Labour came to power in 1974 committed against compulsory policies. The mandarins were most sceptical about what union promises were worth, or about the likelihood that a Labour government under Wilson would be any more successful in controlling pay demands than Edward Heath had been. In June 1975, Harold Wilson made a speech at Stoneleigh which rejected 'panic solutions' to the inflationary problems facing the country in the wake of the oil crisis. Joe Haines, Press Secretary in Harold Wilson's personal staff at No. 10 from 1974 to 1976, wrote:

He was publicly restating his determination to have a voluntary incomes policy which would be acceptable to the people, if not to the Treasury.

While he was at Stoneleigh, things began to happen. Sterling opened at $2.2250 to the £1 that morning and dropped rapidly to $2.1730, or more than 5 cents. The Governor of the Bank, Mr Gordon Richardson, rushed to see the Chancellor. . .

While Harold Wilson was still at Stoneleigh, the Treasury telephoned the private office of No. 10 saying that Richardson and the Chancellor had to see the Prime Minister as soon as he got back. The meeting was arranged to take place at 2.45 p.m. . .

There is no need to speculate about what happened at that meeting. Harold Wilson had heard it all before, when the then Governor of the Bank, Lord Cromer, came to see him in 1964. Selwyn Lloyd, James Callaghan, and Tony Barber had heard it, too, when they were at the Treasury as Chancellors. Sterling was collapsing; unless the drain on the exchanges was stopped there would be a catastrophe; foreign depositors – in this case, the Arabs – were taking out their money; drastic measures, painful but inevitable, had to be taken. The Government had to be seen to be in charge, etc. And what were the drastic measures?

Well, it so happened that the Treasury had them handy. So handy, in fact, that it would be possible for the Cabinet to discuss and endorse them at their meeting next morning. (In breach, incidentally, of the rule that Cabinet papers must be circulated forty-eight hours at least in advance of a Cabinet meeting.) Exceptions can be made in a crisis, however, and this was a crisis. . . And after Cabinet discussion, the Chancellor would be able to announce his measures to the House of Commons that very afternoon, Tuesday July 1st.

Once again, the Home Civil Service (Treasury Division) were throwing the Government a lifebelt when the ship and all hands seemed lost. [15]

Joe Haines recalled that the central element in the package that the Treasury has prepared was a compulsory incomes policy involving a fixed percentage increase of 10%, and legal sanctions against employers. It was already known that the TUC had come to favour the fixed sum increase proposed by Jack Jones, and that this also had large Cabinet support.

> A small group of Ministers, stunned by the suddenness of the crisis, gathered in the Cabinet Room under the Prime Minister's chairmanship. . . They heard the Chancellor's report of the dramatic flight from sterling that had taken place that day and they agreed that a draft statement should be prepared for the Cabinet to consider the next morning before it was delivered at 3.30 p.m. by the Chancellor in the House of Commons. [16]

Bernard Donoughue, head of the Prime Minister's policy unit, and Joe Haines were so suspicious about the coincidence of the run on the pound with the 'moderate' speech – which would have been circulated well in advance around Whitehall – that they decided to wait at No. 10 to see the draft sent across to the Prime Minister by the Treasury. This had been promised for 7 p.m. It arrived at ten minutes past midnight.

> Bernard Donoughue, Janet Hewlett-Davies and I gathered in my office to read it. We were appalled by its tone.
> The Chancellor would be asking Cabinet to consider an unabashed announcement of a statutory incomes policy, with no mention of sanctions against employers – which, if any statutory policy were embarked upon, Ministers insisted was essential – and proposing nothing effective on prices.
> It amounted to a straightforward attempt by the Treasury to make the Government put its policies totally in reverse, abandon its manifesto commitments and commit suicide. [17]

Joe Haines and Bernard Donoughue prepared a counter brief for the Prime Minister that night, emphasizing their suspicion that an attempt to 'stampede' ministers had been made.

> There was one further piece of evidence which had come to us during the evening which strengthened our suspicions about

the behaviour of the Treasury. No attempt had been made by the Treasury and the Bank of England to keep the pound above the crucial $2.20 level. No money had been spent to bolster the rate . . . We had a veritable cornucopia of coincidence.[18]

It is worth noting at this point that wiser counsels and more effective policies than the Treasury's prevailed. The pay policy that was introduced in 1975 was not the Treasury's formulation, but Jack Jones's. It was voluntary, not statutory, and it was extremely successful.

A Treasury man might argue that some such policy had to come in, and that its formulation hardly mattered. If he accepted the version of events that Joe Haines put forward, he might say that something had to force ministers to the point of decision, and that a mini-crisis when officials were ready for it might have been better than a worse crisis when they were unprepared. But it should be further noted that in the time bought by the pay policy, little or nothing was done towards changing Britain's longer-term problems. After the failed initiative of 1976, the crisis came which forced a major change of direction, but in the negative sense.

The example of 1975 shows the Treasury playing what might appear to have been a rather well rehearsed game of 'footsy' with the Bank of England, in building up an atmosphere to stampede ministers into what might or might not be considered sensible policies. The development of British economic policy has been particularly suitable for such a close relationship between the Treasury and the Bank of England. But the cosy relationship between the two was in fact a very old-established one, and the interconnections between the Treasury and the banking community were deeply rooted well before the 1970s.

Sir Otto Niemeyer, who figured prominently in the persuasion of Churchill to the Gold Standard (see Chapter 4) left the Treasury later to become a director of the Bank for International Settlements and a director of the Bank of England. Sir Frederick Leith-Ross (quoted on page 54) who was Deputy Controller of Finance at the Treasury from 1925 to 1932, and Chief Economic Adviser to the government from 1932 to 1946, went on to become Chairman of the Standard Bank, and Deputy Chairman of the National Provincial Bank. As he commented in his memoirs: 'For a few years I also became a director of Babcock and Wilcox and thereby gained some experience of the difficulties of a great manufacturing company: but I gave it up with much regret, as their meetings clashed with those of the National Provincial Bank.'[19] Thus tellingly illustrating the widespread convention among Treasury mandarins that finance comes before the 'real' economy.

Lord Bradbury, who was also an important Civil Service adviser in Churchill's deliberations over the Gold Standard, went on to be President of the British Bankers' Association in 1929.

It would seem that a belief in a 'community of interest' between the banks and the Treasury in the 1920s has continued in somewhat similar form to the present day. The consequences of this for policy in the 1920s will be discussed later. The consequences in post-Second World War Britain seem to have been analogous, in that the interests of manufacturing industry have generally taken a second place when sterling has been threatened. Indeed, in the late 1970s one can see an almost complete return to the pre-1931 Treasury dogma that everything should be sacrificed in the fight to bring inflation down and to protect the financial institutions. Jobs, output, public services – all of these became less important than 'sound finance'.

It may well be argued that interchange between government and industry can risk the development of favouritism between companies, or increase possibilities for corruption. But if the alternative is a thoroughly biased knowledge of a certain sector of the economy, and a high degree of ignorance about the very important remainder which the financial institutions serve, then it would seem worth taking the risk.

At present, the situation is that many great careers in the Civil Service end with exceptionally good positions in financial institutions. At the beginning of 1980, two of the chairmen of the 'big four' clearing banks were former senior officials in government agencies. Sir Jeremy Morse, Chairman of Lloyds Bank, had formerly been a director of the Bank of England. Lord Armstrong, head of the Midland Bank, had formerly been First Permanent Secretary to the Treasury, and head of the Civil Service. Former Treasury Permanent Secretaries tend to gravitate to financial institutions. A move like Alan Lord's to Dunlop in 1977 was an exceptional deviation from the normal progression. Sir Derek Mitchell, who also left the Treasury in 1977, went to Guinness Mahone, the merchant bankers. Sir Douglas Allen, First Permanent

Secretary at the Treasury when Denis Healey became Chancellor and then head of the Civil Service, went on after retirement to become adviser to the Governor of the Bank of England, as well as being a director of the British National Oil Corporation. Interestingly, Sir Douglas Allen (later Lord Croham) called for closer contact between the private sector and Whitehall while he was still head of the Home Civil Service, in an article published in the British Institute of Management's review in early 1977. There is not much evidence that any move towards greater understanding between Whitehall and industry occurred during his distinguished career.

Of course, it may be said that directorships of banks and financial institutions are what ex-senior civil servants are best suited for, especially Treasury men. Yet we have the word of an ex-senior Treasury man to the Radcliffe Committee that it is not financial skills that are most developed at the Treasury, but generalist, intelligent layman skills. It might be thought that these would be useful in a board of directors of any type of company. However there is a distinct tendency for the City to be more attractive than other sectors of industry. This is not in itself sinister. Some social scientists have pointed out the way in which wealth tends to marry wealth, and thus certain social types tend to be particularly closely interlocked. It might well be that similar grounds exist for being unsurprised that Treasury men find future appointments amongst establishments where they have met people with similar social origins and made friendly contacts. As things have stood in Britain for the past fifty years or so, those establishments are most frequently in the City.

When Lawrence Airey took over as Permanent Secretary with responsibility for industrial matters at the Treasury in 1977, the *Sunday Times* reported:

> One rare advantage that Airey brings to his job is that he is a company director of Lord Kearton's British National Oil as well as a civil servant. Though he finds it hard to remember when he last walked round a factory floor he can claim the merit for setting up the regular series of private discussions between Treasury officials and top industrialists. In Great George Street that kind of initiative makes him a revolutionary. [20]

If it was revolutionary in 1977 for a senior Treasury official to have regular discussions with industrialists, we can derive some idea of the level of contact that existed before that time.

The tremendous self-confidence with which the mandarins are at times able to argue their case on an issue is frequently unsupported by any depth of expertise in those particular fields. We have Lord Armstrong's view that senior civil servants did not claim to exercise special skills in fields closely related to the senior posts which they occupied. The rapid movement of civil servants between senior posts ensures that they will not usually accumulate great expertise. The ethic of the brilliant all-rounder still reigns in Whitehall, and the brilliant all-rounders in question are protected by the secrecy of their batting averages. The examples that are discussed elsewhere in this book, relating to major economic issues, point to the danger of having senior secret advisers who are technically as well as practically questionable in their beliefs, with little experience of the real world outside Whitehall's protective walls. As Lord Balogh has commented on civil servants generally:

> In fields in which specialised knowledge or training is required to carry on a sustained argument, the absence of such specialised knowledge invariably leads – not to the absence of theorising, to 'hard-headed realistic empiricism' – but to jejune meditations based on a set of simple theology and beliefs, if not on some long since exploded fallacy. [21]

The ivory tower has indeed changed little over fifty years. The doctrines, the set of simple theology and beliefs that were its currency in 1925, lived on into the 1970s. The 'gold fever' of 1925 and its repercussions apparently taught the inmates little. But the lessons are important. To an increasing extent the inhabitants of Whitehall are becoming regarded as legitimate policy-makers – in sharp contrast to the pre-war doctrine that they were advisers and executors of policy. More and more ministers are reporting difficulties in getting any policy carried out which does not fit in with the view of their senior civil servants.

Meanwhile the ivory tower protects its inmates well. Even gross errors, when made public, appear to be shrugged off easily, with no further comeback. In 1979, for example, it was revealed that the Department of Energy had erroneously paid out £44 million in grants to oil companies. Sir Jack Rampton, the Permanent Secretary at the Department of Energy, said that incorrect claims and officials placing a decimal point in the 'wrong place' had led to the gross error.

Sir Jack said two people had been reprimanded for their part in the affair – an assistant secretary and a principal. What had happened did 'not justify any disciplinary action'. . . Sir Jack was unable to explain to the committee why he had originally told it that an under secretary had been reprimanded.[22]

It is difficult to imagine an erroneous payment of £44 million from private funds being dealt with so casually. The picture created is hardly one which allows easy concurrence with the Boyle Committee's view that security of employment in the public sector compared with the private sector was a relatively minor issue.

The small, exclusive social world of the Treasury mandarin is part of a larger Civil Service cocoon for the administrative élite. A successful career at a private school followed by three years at Oxford or Cambridge, reading an arts subject, leads to entry into that cadre which the 'young flyer' will not leave for forty years or so. During this lifetime of learning his way round Whitehall, never specializing too much in anything, he may well have developed enough contacts to be picked out as a useful adornment to the board of some large financial institution. He will have done many jobs which test his skill in argument – defensive briefs and so on. He will have had to be thorough in his understanding of Whitehall's lines of communication and the sensitivities of officials senior to himself. He will have had to be careful, when working closely with a politician, in private office, not to alienate his political master and to be on his toes and understand Parliament and the media. But he will have been aware that, while political masters come and go, the Treasury influence is permanent. As a Permanent Secretary is said to have remarked to a new Private Secretary in the Chancellor's Private Office: 'Take care of your Chancellor. But remember, your promotion comes from us.'

The viewpoint taken in this world is bound to be influenced by the likely career perspectives and opportunities. The golden road of opportunity for a young official may pass through the Treasury and into the City, but there is no golden road for those who do not identify with the Treasury's view of national interest. To 'cross' the Treasury is indeed a perilous action, even for a senior official

41

elsewhere in Whitehall.

The civil servant might well argue that the Treasury has the best interests of the community at heart, and that its doctrines have been well tried in the past. We shall be examining the impact of some of these doctrines in Chapters 4 and 5 – doctrines applied with miserable effects in the period between the two World Wars, yet recently re-discovered and made fashionable under the cloak of monetarism. The distance of the socially insulated civil servant from the problems of the largest sector of the economy (the manufacturing sector) will be a recurring theme. Edmund Dell, a long-serving economic minister in two governments, has written:

> When businessmen speak to government they normally speak not to ministers but to civil servants. Some businessmen claim to detect in government at the official level an impartiality between British and foreign interests which is difficult to stomach. The Civil Service is believed to constitute a brotherhood so far above the anxieties of ordinary life that it cannot be relied on either for urgency or for commitment to British interests.[23]

When considering the Gold Standard and the rearmament issues, this picture of the 'brotherhood', which Dell holds to be a caricature, is well worth bearing in mind. Good caricatures are, after all, distillations and exaggerations of underlying realities.

Having sketched in some of the social background necessary for an understanding of Treasury officials, it now becomes more illuminating to examine their track record on economic policy. We have an inkling of the sort of golden road along which the mandarins are travelling – but how has this affected the livelihoods of the rest of the United Kingdom? How has their intelligence and knowledge been applied in increasing the national wealth?

Chapter 4 examines a case which comes under the category of the 'fully known' since a great deal of material is available today which throws a startling light on the influence of the officials on policy. The ideas examined throw a very long shadow, however, spanning the time from 'gold fever' in the 1920s all the way to the 1980s. Sixty years have passed, but the doctrines have stayed much the same.

# REFERENCES

1  Sedgemore, Brian, *The Secret Constitution*, Hodder and Stoughton 1980, p.26
2  Roger Berthoud, *The Times*, 6 August 1976
3  Report no. 6 of Review Body on Top Salaries (Chairman Rt Hon. Lord Boyle) December 1974. CMND 5846
4  OECD Main Economic Indicators, September 1975; Annual Abstract Statistics, CSO, 1977
5  *Hansard*, 16 May 1980
6  Expenditure Committee (General Sub-committee), Minutes of Evidence, 5 July 1976, House of Commons, HMSO, 1977
7  Eleventh report from the Expenditure Committee, Minutes of Evidence, vol. 2, part 1. Evidence taken from 3 May to 18 October 1976. Memorandum from the Civil Service Commission, HMSO 1977
8  ibid.
9  Peter Henessy on 'The Ministers and the Mandarins', *Financial Times*, 10 May 1976
10  Roseveare, Henry, *The Treasury – The Evolution of a British Institution,* Allen Lane 1969, p.321
11  *Guardian*, 7 June 1976
12  Roseveare, op. cit., p.321
13  ibid.
14  ibid.
15  Haines, Joe, *The Politics of Power*, Jonathan Cape 1977, pp. 52 – 53
16  Haines, op. cit., p.54
17  Haines, op. cit., p.57
18  Haines, op. cit., pp. 58 – 59
19  Leith-Ross, Sir Frederick, *Money Talks*, Hutchinson 1968, p.341
20  *Sunday Times*, 27 March 1977
21  Balogh, Lord Thomas, in Thomas, Hugh (ed.), *Crisis in the Civil Service*, Anthony Blond 1968, p.17
22  *Financial Times*, 1 November 1979
23  Dell, Edmund, *Political Responsibility and Industry*, George Allen & Unwin 1973, p.146

# 4

# Gold Fever

*The return to gold, in many ways, represented one of the last attempts to apply simple conventional principles to financial and economic problems with a minimum of analysis. The decision and its supposed results largely represented a leap of faith for those involved.*

D.E. Moggridge, The Return to Gold, 1925, *1969*[1]

This chapter is concerned with the illustration of three broad doctrines from pre-war Treasury archives. First, the Treasury's own version of 'gold fever'. Secondly, its resolute refusal to think in terms of the use of resources within the economy, which links closely with the doctrine that budgets always have to balance. Expressed in simple terms, this was sometimes 'we, the government must not try to spend, because spending destroys its own objectives', and sometimes 'we may have the resources, but resources are unreal without any honest money'. The third doctrine is that the only acceptable objective of economic policy is the elimination of inflation. Once prices were brought down, everything else automatically would come right. These identified strands of doctrine are not, of course, independent from one another. Sometimes, elements of one would be used to support another and sometimes the logic would be reversed. Each of them has left its mark on Treasury thinking to this day, and the record shows fairly clearly that not one of the doctrines when applied brought with it the kind of prosperity that was hoped for.

The refusal to think in resource terms led to powerful support being given to appeasement (because Britain could not 'afford' to rearm), and almost calamitously delayed the rearmament programme. The return to gold did not bring with it prosperity or stability internationally. It brought with it lower prices indeed, but contrary to the third doctrine, lower prices tended to depress industry, as the Treasury itself began to argue.

The Treasury, having at first welcomed the crash of 1929 as a forerunner of cheaper credit, blamed what it then acknowledged as the disaster of the depression on falling prices. Thus it carefully stood one of its most cherished doctrines on its head. It seems reasonable to believe that the Treasury's poor pre-war performance, and its negligible role during the war, led to its diminished status just after hostilities ceased. It managed, none the less, to recover its dominance gradually, and even to re-establish some of its pre-war doctrines in modified forms. Instead of the Gold Standard, there is, after 1949, a rigid adherence to a fixed level of sterling against the dollar as a prime symbol of economic virtue. Exaggerated respect for sterling was an emotion shared by many influential politicians.

In place of 'the balanced budget', there existed, for a period, a fundamental acceptance of Keynes's arguments and analysis. But the concentration on inflation as the fundamental target of policy remained, and, in a Keynesian world, the instrument that was chosen to deal with it was pay and wage restraint in some form or other. The advent of Healey marked the partial departure from the objectives of Keynesian policies, and a return to the monetary rhetoric and platitudes of the twenties. The Thatcher government gratefully occupied the seats of monetary orthodoxy so assiduously and unconsciously prepared for them and the clock was turned back to 1925 with the public espousal of a strong pound and a balanced budget. Once more, these were to be the answers to all problems. Co-ordinated intervention, policies on the use of real resources, and planning were not given a serious chance of playing a part in the development of growth in the British economy, despite examples in other, more successful, economies. Furthermore, social trends in British society seemed to militate against the emergence of effective business managers in numbers sufficient to make any impression upon Britain's declining position.

Thus, all Bagehot's cautions about the dangers of bureaucratic government, and its rigidity, were well illustrated by the recrudescence of narrow doctrines within the economic decision-making machinery. The means were thoroughly confused with the end. Contrary to Bagehot's hopes, the presence of fresh inquiring minds at ministerial level did not stop the bureaucratic juggernauts in their relentless courses. As will be seen in the section below, this happened even when a minister with the strength of Churchill posed fundamental questions on policy. Should it seem surprising that politicians in later decades were unable to alter the economic course of the institutions?

One reason for the popularity within the Treasury in the 1920s of a return to gold was a simple bureaucratic one which Bagehot would have appreciated. Gold was what they were used to before the First World War. Returning to gold would be a return to well-remembered habits. But a more powerful motivation was also evident. The City wanted a return to gold, since it was believed this would bring it more business in international finance. Since the Treasury tended in the 1920s, as now, to believe that somehow its main loyalties lay with the City, it is not surprising that they took this special pleading seriously. As R.G. Hawtrey (a leading Treasury theorist of the time) noted in an internal Treasury minute in early 1924:

> In order to re-establish the business of London as a world clearing centre the essential condition is that a sufficient number of foreign currencies should be very nearly fixed in value in relation to sterling...When countries like France, Italy...start the fashion of devaluing their currencies, the transition to a general gold standard may be a very short one, and London may be left isolated with a paper currency in a gold-using world. Should that occur, the danger to the position of London would be aggravated. [2]

This argument was not to the fore when the case was put to Churchill later. However, on more overtly philosophical grounds, all the political parties stood for a return to gold; the Cunliffe Report favoured return, the Imperial Economic Conference favoured return, and the committee which the Labour Chancellor, Philip Snowden, appointed in 1924 (chaired by the ex-Conservative Chancellor, Austen Chamberlain) favoured it. Snowden was a great gold enthusiast, even when he went back into opposition.

Some voices were raised against. The Joint Research and Information Department of the Labour Party and the TUC produced a forceful memo against the possibility of return in 1924:

Whatever may be said in favour of submitting to some measure of deflation in order to secure the advantage of a gold standard, a moment when the trade revival is hesitating, when prices in America are falling and when we are entering on the period of the normal seasonal downward fluctuation in exchange rates, seems a particular inopportune one for putting such a policy into practice. An insistence on a rise in the Bank Rate at the present time, whatever may be said for it in the long run, looks very much like a sacrifice of the immediate interests of the general public to the immediate interests of the bankers.[3]

The memo made forceful comments on the rise in unemployment that return to gold at the old par rate would entail.

The prohibition on the export of gold, which was a crucial part of being a 'paper' currency, rather than a Gold Standard currency, was due to expire on 31 December 1925. Winston Churchill had entered Cabinet as Chancellor of the Exchequer after the Conservatives' landslide victory in October 1924. Otto Niemeyer, Controller of Finance at the Treasury, briefed Churchill on the pressing needs to return to gold. Various different governments had expressed their intention to return, he argued. The expectation of return was so strong that a failure to return at the opportunity offered by the export of gold legislation would cause a sterling crisis. Failure to return to gold was anathema:

It would reverberate throughout a world which has not forgotten the uneasy moments of the winter of 1923 ... The immediate consequences would be a considerable withdrawal of balances and investment (both foreign *and British*) from London; a heavy drop in Exchange; and to counteract that tendency, a substantial increase in Bank rate ...

Apart from one or two theoretical advocates of a 'managed currency' there is no body of opinion, either financial or industrial, in this country which does not wish for the restoration of the gold standard.[4]

Sensitive of the criticism that the move would favour banks unduly, Niemeyer argued that banks were favoured by cheap money. He accepted that the return would raise interest rates, although this would mean only a 'temporary increase' in Bank Rate. He also admitted that there were fears (outside the Treasury) of the effect of higher interest rates on trade and employment. But since, in the long run, Niemeyer asserted that it would be better for trade to

47

return to gold, it must also be better for employment in the long run. 'The real antithesis is between the long view and the short view. Bankers on the whole take longer views than manufacturers. But the view is of what is good for trade and industry as a whole, on which after all the banks entirely depend, not of what may enable the bank to bleed its traders.'[5]

Niemeyer omitted to note that if the London Bank was expanding its business on the basis of trade between third party countries, for instance between Sweden and Germany, then its interests would become completely detached from the interests of the British manufacturer. Indeed, as can be seen from the Treasury minute written in 1924, it was the expansion of this type of business that particularly interested the Treasury, all part of the re-establishment of the City as a 'world centre' of finance. This aspect of the return to gold was very much played down in Niemeyer's note to the Chancellor quoted above.

Churchill was less dismissive of the views of critics of the Gold Standard than were his civil servants. Setting forth a number of problems which he foresaw in the return to gold (in a memorandum to be entitled 'The Exercise' in the Treasury) Churchill re-asserted that the interests of different sectors of the economy did not perfectly coincide:

> The whole question of a return to the Gold Standard must not be dealt with only upon its financial and currency aspects. The merchant, the manufacturer, the workman and the consumer have interests which, though largely common, do not by any means exactly coincide either with each other or with the financial and currency interests...If the Government took positive action to restore the Gold Standard and this were followed by a rise in the Bank Rate, we should certainly be accused of having favoured the special interests of finance at the expense of the special interests of production.[6]

Churchill resisted being bullied over the lapse in gold export legislation later that year, commenting that it could be renewed for two or three years. He requested plain and solid advantages of the policy to be presented, and also a reply to the question, 'Why then should we not continue on the basis of a managed finance?'[7] Hawtrey, Niemeyer, the Governor, and Bradbury set about replying to the Chancellor's question. Bradbury was more than a little contemptuous of Churchill's anxiety. He wrote a little covering note as his contribution in response to Churchill: 'The writer of the memorandum appears to have his spiritual home in the Keynes-McKenna sanctuary, but some of the trimmings of his mantle have been furnished by the "Daily Express".'[8] In his more analytical memorandum, he argued that failure to return to gold would lead to a fall in the value of the pound and that this would lead to the need for a tough credit squeeze. This would be the necessary policy according to the scientific advocates of the 'managed' pound, he claimed. However, the covering note to Niemeyer suggested that Niemeyer should play on Churchill's obvious distaste for a higher interest rate and the creation of unemployment by emphasizing that the 'Keynes-McKenna creed' would require worse restrictions than gold orthodoxy.

Montagu Norman, in his reply to the questions set by Churchill, reacted tetchily to the idea that plain solid answers for the ordinary man should be found and shown: 'In connection with a golden 1925, the merchant, manufacturer, workman, etc., should be considered (but not consulted any more than about the design of battleships).'[9] He also played on Churchill's anxiety over higher interest rates by suggesting that if a return to gold were delayed, interest rates in London would be higher than otherwise. His reasons, hinted at rather than explicit, were different from Bradbury's. A greater demand for loans in London seemed to be his explanation to the Chancellor for the need for interest rates to be higher in London even with a 'golden 1925'.

Churchill's anxiety over the division between financial and industrial interests was answered on 2 February by Niemeyer. He argued that, 'The banker has little desire for dear money', contrary to common belief. The fact that the Governor was pointing out the necessity of higher interest rates in the future, with the return to gold, does not seem to have worried the officials unduly. The answer, at least for their debating purposes, was that the anti-gold experts would want higher interest rates too. Naturally, the anti-gold Keynes-McKenna apostles were not able to state their own case blow by blow in the proceedings, and the Chancellor was invited to believe the Bradbury-Niemeyer view of what Keynes and McKenna might argue.

Hawtrey argued that returning to gold would restore stability of exchanges, and thus of trade. Trade had been damaged by the absence of a Gold Standard over the six years since the First World War, claimed Hawtrey, although he produced no figure to justify this. He reiterated, in a rather diluted form, the arguments for a return to gold that he had put in his memo for Niemeyer the year before. Instead of its being in London's interest, 'It is emphatically a British interest that the pre-war system should be restored. But it is incidentally also a world-wide interest.'[10]

Throughout the material submitted to the Chancellor and assembled by Niemeyer, there is a detectable undercurrent of the sentiment that only a fool could refuse to do what was advised – as in Norman's submission: 'Gold is the guarantee of good faith. . . The only possible alternative to Gold was a price level scheme (Irving Fisher and others). Now there *is* no alternative to Gold in the opinion of educated and reasonable men.'[11] Despite this kind of invitation to show that he was an educated and reasonable man, Churchill continued to have the courage to express doubts about whether the emperor had clothes or not.

It seems that Churchill asked in late February for comments on an article on gold sent to him by the author, J.St Loe Strachey. Comments on this article were exchanged between Niemeyer and two more junior Treasury officials, Messrs Young and Rowe Dutton. The officials argued that the world was not in need of greater fixed capital: '. . .it is at least arguable that we have far too much fixed capital: factories, plant, ships, etc., etc.'[12] This particular sentiment is strangely at odds with the other Treasury view expressed later in the 1930s that there were no resources to spare, for instance, to allow rearmament. J.M. Keynes sent the Chancellor a copy of an article which he had published in *The Nation* at the end of February. Niemeyer's criticism of Keynes for Churchill's edification began: 'Unlike many other journalists, Mr Keynes is a serious critic of monetary policy.'[13] He lost no opportunity to denigrate Keynes: 'when two years ago Bank rate was raised from 3% to 4% Keynes prophesied blue ruin (which did not occur). . . The history of the last two years (during which we have waited for the prophecies of Keynes' school about the United States to come true). . . All the news we get from the United States (where Keynes has not been recently). . .'[14] In this particular briefing, Niemeyer became much more frank about one particular advantage of the return to gold, the advantage to the City: 'How are we to maintain entrepôt financial business, when no foreigner knows what a £ will cost him, and how are we to make foreign loans when no borrower knows how much he is going to repay?'

Keynes's article, published on 21 February 1925, emphasized the terrible risks of being shackled through gold to the more volatile and dynamic US economy, as well as the risks of higher interest rates and deflation:

> What solid advantages will there be to set against these risks? I do not know. Our bankers speak of 'psychological' advantages. But it will be poor consolation that 'nine people out of ten' expected advantages, if none in fact arrive.
>
> That our Bank chairmen should have nothing better to cry than 'Back to 1914' and that they should believe that this represents the best attainable, is not satisfactory. The majority of those who are studying the matter are becoming agreed that faults in our credit system are at least partly responsible for the confusions which result in the paradox of unemployment amidst dearth. [15]

Keynes thus turned the debate to be an attack on that most hallowed ground from the Treasury viewpoint, the City itself.

Churchill was clearly unimpressed by Niemeyer's instant response, and wrote to him on 22 February:

> The Treasury have never, it seems to me, faced the profound significance of what Keynes calls 'the paradox of unemployment amidst dearth'. The Governor shows himself perfectly happy in the spectacle of Britain possessing the finest credit in the world simultaneously with a million and a quarter unemployed. Obviously if these million and a quarter were usefully and economically employed, they would produce at least £100 a year a head, instead of costing us at least £50 a year a head in doles. We should have at least £200 millions a year healthy net increase. These figures are of course purely illustrative. It is impossible not to regard such an object as at least equal, and probably superior, to the other valuable objectives you mention on your last page. The community lacks goods, and a million and a quarter people lack work. It is certainly one of the highest functions of national finance and credit to bridge the gulf between the two.
>
> This is the only country in the world where this condition exists. The Treasury and the Bank of England policy has been the only policy consistently pursued. It is a terrible responsibility for those who have shaped it, unless they can be sure that there is no connection between the unique British

phenomenon of chronic unemployment and the long resolute consistency of a particular financial policy. I do not know whether France with her financial embarrassments can be said to be worse off than England with her unemployment. At any rate while that unemployment exists, no one is entitled to plume himself on the financial or credit policy which we have pursued.

It may be of course that you will argue that unemployment would have been much greater but for the financial policy pursued; that there is no sufficient demand for commodities either internally or externally to require the services of this million and a quarter people; that there is nothing for them but to hang like a millstone round the neck of industry and on the public revenue until they become permanently demoralised. You may be right, but if so, it is one of the most sombre conclusions ever reached. On the other hand I do not pretend to see even 'through a glass darkly' how the financial and credit policy of the country could be handled so as to bridge the gap between a dearth of goods and a surplus of labour; and well I realise the danger of experiment to that end. The seas of history are full of famous wrecks. Still if I would rather see Finance less proud and Industry more content.

You and the Governor have managed this affair. Taken together I expect you know more about it than anyone else in the world. At any rate alone in the world you have had an opportunity over a definite period of years of seeing your policy carried out. That is a great policy, greatly pursued, I have no doubt. But the fact that this island with its enormous extraneous resources is unable to maintain its population is surely a cause for the deepest heart searching. Forgive me adding to your labours by these Sunday morning reflections.[16]

Niemeyer replied:

Does the paradox of unemployment amidst dearth arise wholly or mainly from credit policy? Clearly not wholly. One obvious cause of the paradox is maladjustment of labour supplies. There is a dearth of houses because of houses depend on the supply of certain skilled labourers and these skilled labourers may not be recruited or diluted from the unemployed of other trades. Or there is a dearth of trade in parts of Europe because transit conditions or tariffs do not permit goods to arrive sufficiently expeditiously or even at all.

I doubt whether credit policy is even a chief cause, and I at any rate would not advocate, still less be 'happy' with a credit policy which I thought would produce unemployment. What does one mean by 'usefully and economically employed?' Surely employed not merely in producing goods but in producing goods that can be disposed of to others? You can by inflation (a most vicious form of subsidy) enable, temporarily, spending power to cope with large quantities of products. But unless you increase the dose continually, there comes a time when having destroyed the credit of the country you can inflate no more, money having ceased to be acceptable as value. Even before this, as your inflated spending power creates demand, you have had claims for increased wages, strikes, lock outsss etc. I assume it to be admitted that with Germany and Russia before us we do not think plenty can be found on this path.[17]

It is very clear what a totally static world the Treasury lived in at that time. There was no concept of productivity improvements being generated by growth, which might offset long-run tendencies to higher prices. Niemeyer did not really answer the basic point about unemployment being the natural result of government restrictive policies that would need to go hand in hand with the Gold Standard. His explanation of the reason for existing unemployment was particularly glib. No doubt some labour was in short supply, and demand to an extent was mismatched with supply, but presumably willingness to train and adapt on the part of industrialists was also related to availability of credit, and industrialists' anticipation of the strength of demand.

It is especially interesting in Niemeyer's argument to notice that he admitted the possibility that demand could be expanded – but then even more terrible things would happen, with workers asking for more wages and the path would be set for red revolution. The Treasury thus had a dim idea that the level of unemployment was a sort of cushion against such pressures. Moreover, there is little or no evidence that the Treasury cared much about the unemployed, certainly not if they stood in the way of a 'golden 1925'. Only a few years before, the Treasury had put a note to the Cabinet Committee on Unemployment which contained the memorable recommendation that the unemployed should be kept on the verge of starvation.[18]

Churchill's humanity was in no doubt, however, nor his common sense, compared with the almost feverish tone of the officials pushing him towards gold. It was clear that Churchill was still not convinced of the arguments put by Niemeyer *et al*. He arranged a dinner in March, which confronted Niemeyer and Lord Bradbury with the two leading critics of their orthodoxy, Keynes and McKenna. It appears that McKenna finally supported the view that Churchill was obliged to go ahead with the return on *political* grounds, although he felt it was a ghastly mistake from the point of view of sensible economic policy. Very soon after this dinner, Churchill decided that he would announce the return to the Gold Standard.

A significant sidelight is thrown upon this final decision by Sir Frederick Leith-Ross in his memoirs. Leith-Ross was a senior Treasury official in 1925, becoming Deputy Controller of Finance in that year.

> The Chancellor finally decided in favour of the return to gold – partly, as he himself said, because he knew that if he adopted this course Niemeyer would give him irrefutable arguments to support it, whereas if he refused to adopt it he would be faced with criticisms from the City authorities against which he would not have any effective answer. In fact, Winston later claimed that the return to gold, by giving stability of prices, improved the standard of living of the people – at least of the great majority who were employed.[19]

Having made the decision, it was only natural that any politician with an instinct for survival should point out the beneficial results, at least to those who were employed. As was inevitable, the Bank Rate had to be raised from 4% to 5% in March. It went up before the announcement of the return to head off the inevitable *post hoc ergo propter hoc* argument should the rate have moved up after the return. This was Churchill's idea.

Unemployment rose sharply in 1926, and the return to gold made its own substantial contribution to the stagnation of the British economy in the years up to 1929. Furthermore, class bitterness and massive disruption were inflamed by the consequent downward pressures on wages. In 1931 the Labour government failed to achieve unanimity on ultra deflationary policies – considered, naturally enough, largely on the grounds that they were needed to stabilize the foreign exchange position. The government fell. The incoming National government was pressurized into taking Britain off gold in September 1931, by forces greater than the arguments of Montagu Norman and the like. Niemeyer was out of the Treasury by that time, and in 1931 (the year the pound fell) was elevated to the post of Director, at the Bank for International Settlements in Switzerland.

The return to gold had been a disastrous policy. It was not only criticized bitterly by economic authors such as Keynes. A modern economic historian has commented:

> As far as 1925 conditions were concerned, the pound was now (after the return to gold) markedly overvalued, and in consequence exports were further discouraged and the export industries hit again, imports were encouraged, the balance of payments was adversely affected and the pound weakened still more, so that restrictive and deflationary policies had to continue to prevent an outflow of gold and a collapse of sterling.'[20]

From 1925 to 1931, the money incomes of those in employment in manufacturing fell by 3% (although with the fall in prices, real incomes grew slowly). Unemployment went up from 1,200,000 in 1925 to 1,380,000 in 1926. After falling in 1927, unemployment once more rose, to reach a monthly average of 2,600,000 in 1931, as the world recession bit deeply into the economy. Iron and steel output only exceeded the level reached in 1923 in one year, 1929. Industrial production moved erratically, and net real investment in manufacturing never regained the level it had reached in 1925. Who really gained from the return to gold? London became a massive centre for short-term funds. As the American economist Leland Yeager has commented:

> In fact an abnormally large volume of international short-term money existed in the late 1920s, ready to flit from one financial centre to another as risks and earnings opportunities changed. Before the crisis of 1931, London harboured much of these funds. The advantage of having foreign balances in London was shaky. If they should be quickly withdrawn, as finally did happen, a house of cards would come tumbling down.[21]

But, of course, in the years before the house of cards crashed, the financial intermediaries in the City of London could be making comfortable incomes for themselves, despite the fact that the British economy was stagnating. As Yeager puts it: 'Superficially, though, it might seem a benefit that the "City" of London, while never regaining its unchallenged pre-war supremacy, did regain the prestige of a gold standard centre and did attact short-term foreign funds in heavier volume than before the war.'[22]

Churchill's stated objective of seeing 'Finance less proud and Industry more content' was therefore actively negated by the policy which his officials recommended to him. His basic arguments were not answered, other than with platitudes and sophistry. Furthermore, Britain was put on a course which ill-prepared her for the tests of the following decade. The chosen doctrine of the bureaucrats had prevailed. It is impossible to believe that Churchill took that momentous decision simply on the grounds that 'Niemeyer and company would brief him well' as suggested by Leith-Ross. And clearly, Churchill did recognize it to be a momentous decision. Yet the arguments put to him by the officials were never scrutinized by those outside the machine. The officials could secretly denigrate the published arguments of outside critics like Keynes – but Keynes could not see their criticism and fight on equal terms. An issue which involves potential gain for speculators has to be shrouded in secrecy to an extent – but for the system to work effectively it is also necessary that the advisers should not have an exaggerated bias – in this case, in favour of the narrow interests of the City of London. The City had a legitimate right, as would any other productive sector of the economy, to push for its own case to be heard. But the Treasury, as the policy-making body for the whole economy, should have carefully balanced those interests against the interests of other sectors, particularly manufacturing industry. One strong minister was clearly insufficient in this case to offset the inherent dangers of the inbred bureaucratic world of the Treasury, with windows ever facing the Bank of England.

The 'gold fever' in the Treasury did not die, as might have been expected, with the collapse of the world financial system in the early 1930s. A non-expert in financial matters might have imagined that a failure on that scale showed there was something wrong with the practice of rigidly binding national currencies to gold. The 'experts' in the Treasury, however, still continued to hanker after gold, and after greater freedom for world trade and capital. As late as 1937, when world economic activity and employment had been

# Table 5: *British unemployment, industrial production and prices, 1922–39*[23]

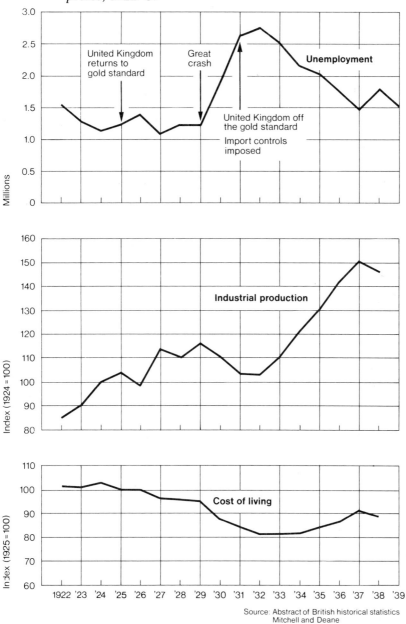

Source: Abstract of British historical statistics
Mitchell and Deane

recovering at a tremendous rate after the imposition of import controls and tariffs around the globe, Whitehall's Committee on Economic Information presented a long report to Cabinet, which in part concluded:

> Yet the prosperity of this country more than that of any other is bound up with the revival of international trade, and if it were true that a restoration of some sort of international gold standard is a condition of any large relaxation of trade barriers, and would in fact secure such relaxation, we, of all countries, should be prepared to examine the question. [24]

This particular paper on economic prospects contained a lengthy theoretical international finance section, including the sentence above, although figures elsewhere in the report clearly indicated the scale of world recovery at the time in the absence of either free trade or the Gold Standard. In 1937, world trade in volume terms was still 1.7% below the level reached in 1929 (the crest of the pre-depression boom) but the latest figures in the report showed it over 17% ahead of the year before. Output in the US, France and Germany was well ahead of the 1936 levels. In the UK the report showed that the output of steel was running at over double the rate it had fallen to in the worst of the recession, and retail sales were around 20% ahead of the depression levels. Other indices of output, produced much later, indicate that in 1937 industrial production in Britain was about 30% above the level attained in 1929. [25] The chart on page 57 illustrates dramatically the revival of industrial output after 1931, and the consequent fall in unemployment. From 1932 to 1937, unemployment fell by over one million. The 'gold bugs' would perhaps point to the success in price reduction from 1925 to 1931 – the price of that success is also clear.

The basic statistics of the time showed that Britain's prosperity was enormously increased without the free trade and Gold Standard that the doctrinaires were calling for so nostalgically – Britain had never in her history reached the level of output attained in 1937. Unemployment had sunk to the lowest level in six years, and average real incomes were over 10% higher than they had been in the brief 'second golden age', 1925-31. The argument that Britain's prosperity was bound up with the revival of international trade should therefore have seemed preposterous to anyone reading it at the time who kept abreast of real industrial life in Britain. One group in Britain might have been feeling the pinch, however. Any banker who had earned a good living out of financing third party trade, trade between other countries, in the buoyant twenties, might well have been looking back wistfully to his own, personal golden age. As the report made clear: 'Finally, the return to fixed parities would facilitate the resumption of international lending for the financing of trade on an important scale.' It is evident, however, from the committee's report that the orthodox views were not universal. Keynes's presence as an 'outside' adviser may be the reason for the cautious tone of some paragraphs:

*They were virtually all outside advisers*

> On the other side there are substantial arguments against a return to a regime of fixed parities. First, this is a course which we have in general opposed hitherto, on the grounds that (i) it would involve some renunciation of our liberty of action in the matter of credit policy, and (ii) it would imply that any diverging tendencies between British and international prices would call for correction through the cumbrous method of influencing the internal price level.[26]

After eighteen dense pages of argument and counter argument, the only practical proposal that the committee made was that the Bank of England should quote buying and selling prices for gold, and that other central banks should do the same. If Cabinet had not had other weighty matters on its agenda, many unproductive headaches might have been generated by this document.

The conclusion which seems to come from the events described above is that when the Treasury shared a doctrine with the Bank of England which was in the specific interests of one sector of the City, that policy was pursued vigorously. Only a total international financial collapse was sufficient to dislodge the policy in question. When, contrary to the doctrine, international prosperity began to return, the doctrinaires refused to refer to the actual available statistical material and argued once more a case 'for the general good' that would once more favour the traditional interest group within the City. At the same time they admitted that this would possibly be detrimental to freedom of economic decision-making.

Even though the mandarins might still be pining for the golden age in the 1930s, having witnessed the calamitous depression and the disintegration of their dreams on an international scale, this did not prevent them from continuing to attempt to apply other aspects of the creed at home.

The consequences this was to have on Britain's place in world politics, particularly on Britain's state of armed readiness, is the topic of the following chapter.

REFERENCES

1 Moggridge, D.E., *The Return to Gold, 1925*, Cambridge University Press 1969, p.89
2 T176/5, 26 April 1924, R.G. Hawtrey
3 Norton, J.E., TUC/Labour Party Joint Research and Information Department Paper No. 34, June 1924. In T176/5
4 T172/1499 B. Otto Niemeyer's covering note for Churchill to the Austen Chamberlain Committee draft report
5 ibid.
6 T172/1499B, 29 January 1925. W.S. Churchill
7 ibid.
8 T172/1499B, 5 February 1925. Lord Bradbury
9 T172/1499B, Montagu Norman
10 T172/1499B, 2 February 1925. R.G. Hawtrey
11 T172/1499B, 2 February 1925
12 T172/1499B, 12 February 1925. Comments on J. St Loe Strachey's letter and attachments
13 T172/1499B, 21 February 1925
14 ibid.
15 Keynes, J.M., *The Nation and the Atheneum*, 21 February 1925
16 T172/1499B, 22 February 1925. W.S. Churchill
17 T172/1499B, O. Niemeyer to W.S. Churchill
18 CAB 27/229, 26 September 1921
19 Leith-Ross, Sir Frederick, *Money Talks*, Hutchinson 1968, p.92
20 Pollard, Sidney, *The Gold Standard and Employment Policies Between the Wars*, University Paperbacks 1970, Introduction, p.3
21 Yeager, Leland, *International Monetary Relations*, Harper and Row 1966, pp. 279–80
22 Yeager, op. cit., p.279

23 Mitchell, B.R. and Deane, P., *Abstract of British Historical Statistics*, Cambridge University Press 1962
24 CAB 24/273, 25 November 1937. Report of the Committee on Economic Information
25 The Lomax index, in Mitchell and Deane, op. cit., p.272
26 CAB 24/273, op. cit.

Drawing partly on Henson oW inch?

# 5

# From Resisting Rearmament to Planning

*At the beginning of the rearmament campaign it was laid down that full Treasury control over expenditure was to be maintained, and the result has been delays and difficulties at every stage.*
Rt Hon. *Alfred Duff Cooper DSO, shortly after resigning as First Lord of the Admiralty, 1938*[1]

*...and it is not pushing speculation beyond legitimate lengths to infer that the Government, though on the one hand determined to carry on with their policy of national defence, anticipate on the other hand a rich harvest of industrial confidence from their policy of international appeasement and of promoting the revival of international trade.*
The Times, *Editorial, 26 February 1938*[2]

*The conflict between the armed services and the Treasury was the focal point of the debate within the government over rearmament policy. In this conflict the emergence of first Japan and then Germany as military threats gave the services more than ample material to buttress their cases for expansion. Their lack of unity, however, precluded the possibility of their developing a coherent program and diminished the impact of their proposals to the Cabinet. This enabled the Treasury to forward its own policies by playing the services off against one another. Although the military threat to Britain provided a powerful impetus to rearm, the services were unable to prevail on the Cabinet to insure that the nation's defences were adequate.*
*Robert Paul Shay,* British Rearmament in the Thirties, *1977*[3]

The issues of rearmament in the 1930s once more brought common sense into collision with Treasury dogma. The most persuasive and influential cluster of dogmas governing Treasury thought in the 1920s and 1930s flowed from the abstract theory of static economics, developed by the 'classical' economic school. It is impossible to name one author who can be pointed to as the cardinal exponent of the classical theory. Keynes himself, in criticizing the policy prescriptions which had been drawn from the classical school had to summarize the 'basic case' at the outset of his critique in *The General Theory of Employment, Interest and Money*. The classical economists have a lineage dating from Adam Smith in the eighteenth century, through J.S. Mill and Ricardo in the nineteenth century to their followers such as Pigou in the twentieth century. The pure theory is not the focus of attention in this book. Its interpretation into crude rules for government action is of interest, however – in particular the degeneration of an isolated number of conclusions into dogmas which were put to politicians as absolute truths.

Two dogmas which pervaded Treasury thinking between the two World Wars related to the use of economic resources, and to the role which government spending had in affecting the development of the economy as a whole. Firstly, the Treasury believed that government spending was in itself destructive of underlying economic resources. Secondly, they believed that all unemployment was caused by wage levels being too high. Both of these dogmas live on in various guises, and crop up in various parts of this book, mouthed by a wide variety of political figures at various points of historical convenience or exigence.

It was probably very comfortable for the consciences of policy-makers to hold the second of these beliefs, since its logical consequence was that the unemployed had only themselves to blame for their predicament. Furthermore, if you also believed that government spending destroyed resources, it was inevitable that you would argue against helping the unemployed with any Exchequer funds. The unemployed themselves were not regarded by the bureaucrats as an 'unused resource'. As we saw earlier, it was only Churchill and 'outsiders' who thought in those terms. If you held to the rigid dogma, no real sacrifice was being made by the economy if the entrepreneurs did not wish to hire more labour.

For the Treasury mandarin in the 1920s, inflation seemed a much bigger threat than unemployment. We might further reflect that whereas inflation would affect him, unemployment would not. Nevertheless, 'sound currency' was regarded as his responsibility, and he believed that the creation of wealth and use of resources was the affair of the entrepreneur. The bankers, furthermore, would argue that the entrepreneur needed stable prices for his success. Behind these beliefs lay a generally tacit assumption that the total output of the economy was unaffected by government policy, and broadly, that it was static. Statistical information was so limited in the early twenties that the Treasury had no idea what the proportionate relationship was between government spending and total national output.

In 1920, a Treasury paper was circulated to the Cabinet Committee on Unemployment which, while emphasizing how the Treasury had been bending its principles in order to smooth the adjustments necessary after the First World War, still pointed to the need to economize. The Treasury attached a paper written by Professor Gustav Cassel in support of their view that public spending would create more inflation. Cassel's text warned strongly against intervention by the state: 'The danger is then that the Government, under the influence of false philanthropic ideas, feels itself obliged to subsidise the labourers brought under this pressure, offering them unemployment doles or starting comprehensive schemes of construction works, in order to create employment...'[4]

The pressure which the labourers would be under without state help would force them to take lower wages. The Treasury explained this more clearly in a note by the Chancellor, Sir Robert Horne, to the same committee in 1921:

The root cause of unemployment at the present time (so far as it is not due to wilful destruction of mines etc.) is that the costs of production are so high that purchasers whether from abroad or in this country cannot afford to buy. The main item in the cost of production is the cost of wages. The only hope of ultimate full employment in this country is therefore a reduction in prices and correspondingly in wages. Any step which by artificial credit maintains prices is likely to mean an ultimate increase in unemployment... Relief of unemployment results therefore in buying small present ease at increased cost in the very near future...[5]

It should be noted that a Chancellor's Cabinet papers, being so numerous, are most frequently written by officials and signed by the incumbent with little modification.

The dogma was taken to the point at which the implied pressure on the unemployed recommended by the Treasury was greater than that achieved by German submarines in the lately finished war: 'The national financial position makes it therefore imperative to limit assistance for unemployment to something near the barest minimum needed to prevent starvation.'[6]

On that occasion the Treasury writers of the Chancellor's paper felt no need at all to economize in their tour of dogmas and platitudes: 'If this country is to be restored to its pre-war position, it is essential that its industry, banking and commerce should act independently of the State.'[7]So any state intervention was believed to militate against recovery.

It is interesting to note that while unemployment shot up in 1921, and continued rising in 1922 to reach a level of over one and a half million in that year, money wage rates had begun to fall steeply at the beginning of 1921. The fall in weekly money wages in 1921 was no less than 22%. [8] The Treasury never appeared to feel it was necessary to refer to statistical evidence in support of its assertions in these cases however. The assertions were so self evident to reasonable men.

After the new golden age had failed to ensure increased output and employment, the Treasury was obliged to re-think some of the basic elements of the doctrines we have seen above. The crash of 1929, and the recession of the early 1930s induced the mandarins to turn one doctrine on its head. By 1937, the Treasury experts had come to believe that the depression had been caused, intensified and prolonged by *falling* prices. Price inflation therefore began to be equated with *increasing* prosperity:

> We are now back to the 1930 price level with every prospect that in about a year we may be back at a price level similar to that of 1929 and 1928 and say 40 per cent higher than the price level of 1931. That is what we have wanted and it should on the whole mean prosperity. [9]

This comment was made by a senior Treasury official in a briefing note for Sir Richard Hopkins, in the late 1930s. Nevertheless, such a total conversion could not be effected without certain misgivings:

> We shall be very naive if we think that the rise will proceed

up to the level we want and then stop. The rise in prices will not stop itself. Just as during the slump the fall in one price led to the fall in others with cumulative depressing effects, so during the boom the rise in one price leads to the rise of others continually. [10]

Despite this reversal of view on prices, the Treasury view on actual government expenditure remained steadfast through the thirties. While Germany rearmed, the Treasury implacably opposed increasing British spending on its defensive forces. As we have noted, one aspect of the doctrinaire opposition to public spending was the resolute belief that public spending could never actually increase the sum of goods produced by society. In other words, if the government spent money on some project or other, an equivalent amount of desired economic activity elsewhere in the economy would automatically have to be stopped. At the same time, whatever was performed through public spending would be self defeating.

As unemployment rose in 1921, and as greater pressure was brought to bear on politicians in government to do something, the doctrinaire advice was that action would be futile:'An artificial stimulation of the home demand will merely mean encouraging people in this country to take in each other's washing and waste their energies in so doing.'[11]

It was Keynes who introduced the revolutionary concept that a government could actually affect the total sum of economic activity without introducing financial chaos in the process. The Treasury, naturally enough, resisted Keynes's notions, which had been given a partial airing in the Liberal Party campaign for more intervention on the part of government to deal with unemployment. With Keynes's help, the Liberals produced a pamphlet in 1929, entitled boldly 'We Can Conquer Unemployment', and argued that it could be financially sound to launch their programme. Officials in the Department of Labour were clearly a little concerned at the implications of the pamphlet. As one official commented:

There is, however, one important point to which a convincing public answer is necessary, and that is the financial basis.

Many prophets have pointed out that 'here are the unemployed, and here is the work that needs to be done'. (Squeers was one of the first.) The pamphlet says, in addition, 'here is the money'.

...The point is not one for the Ministry of Labour, but obviously if the pamphlet or the Theory is right, the case for the programme is immensely strengthened. It may be moonshine (it seems so to me) but if so, the Treasury ought to dispose of it. [12]

A coherent Treasury rebuttal of the arguments has proved difficult to find. However, the Public Records Office has noted that the Treasury copy of the pamphlet has 'EXTRAVAGANCE INFLATION BANKRUPTCY' scrawled across it. [13] At a more sophisticated level, we do have the Treasury's comments on Keynes's theories. His *The General Theory of Employment, Interest and Money* was first published in February 1936. In it he showed at the theoretical level how it was possible for government policy to affect the level of unemployment, and how policies towards higher interest rates could actually depress the level of activity in the economy and also the level of investment. Keynes knew that his conclusions would be politically distasteful to some; particularly since he was calling for greater government involvement in the running of the economy:

Our criticism of the accepted classical theory of economics has consisted not so much in finding logical flaws in its analysis as in pointing out that its tacit assumptions are seldom or never satisfied, with the result that it cannot solve the economic problems of the actual world...Whilst, therefore, the enlargement of the functions of government, involved in the task of adjusting to one another the propensity to consume and the inducement to invest, would seem to a nineteenth-century publicist or to a contemporary American financier to be a terrific encroachment on individualism, I defend it, on the contrary both as the only practicable means of avoiding the destruction of existing economic forms in their entirety and as the condition of the successful functioning of individual initiative.

For if effective demand is deficient, not only is the public scandal of wasted resources intolerable, but the individual enterpriser who seeks to bring these resources into action is operating with the odds loaded against him. [14]

R.G. Hawtrey at the Treasury, quickly wrote a brief for the edification of other Treasury officials, which naturally attacked the new theory: 'The idea that a tendency for investment and saving to become different has to be counteracted by an expansion or contraction of the total of incomes is an absurdity; such a tendency cannot strain the economic system, it can only strain Mr Keynes's vocabulary.'[15]

A set of dogmas which led to the unemployed being kept on the brink of starvation, that assisted in making the recession as deep as it was, and which kept British industry on average more depressed than industry in other nations might be regarded as pernicious enough. The purblind arrogance of the officials who put forward these doctrines might be regarded, with the benefit of hindsight, as particularly objectionable. But in the period up to the Second World War, the doctrines which we have mentioned had a further and almost fatal consequence for the British nation. The belief that budgets had to be balanced to maintain sound finance, and that government spending actually destroyed resources, led the leading Treasury mandarins to oppose rearmament bitterly. Cabinet minutes of the period show the extent to which Chancellors were briefed to intervene in a wide range of matters, even on foreign affairs, in any way which seemed expedient, if the objective was that of diminishing the perceived need to increase military preparedness.

When deficiencies in the defence departments were noted by ministers in early 1933, the Chancellor of the Exchequer, Neville Chamberlain, stated the Treasury line that 'financial and economic risks are by far the most serious and urgent that the country has to face, and that other risks have to be run until the country has had time and opportunity to recuperate and our financial situation to improve'[16] In 1934, after Winston Churchill had started what was to be an epic campaign to persuade government to bring the air force up to an adequate standard, the Chancellor argued once more in Cabinet that the raising of extra finance for defence departments was 'the broad road that led to destruction'. [17]

The funds in question were £70 million spread over five years, for reaching effective strength. It is worth noting that spread over such a period this was equivalent to less than 2% of government expenditure at the time. In terms of under-utilized resources, over two million were unemployed on average in 1934, and steel output was 8% lower than it had been in 1929. There was no argument on common sense grounds that national resources were overstretched, therefore. The case was quite the opposite.

Seven months later, in 1935, the Treasury had disturbing

intelligence placed before it: Germany was mobilizing resources for rearmament on a massive scale. It was known that Germany was rearming, but the figures shook officials. The British Embassy in Berlin confirmed to Warren Fisher that Germany had raised the equivalent of £880 million in the previous two years, by means of a floating debt. Over half this was estimated by the Embassy staff to be going towards armaments programmes, and the rest towards unemployment schemes and export subsidies. The German plans were to raise the allocation steeply over the two forthcoming years. The covering Treasury remarks on the Embassy paper noted that in the longer run, such methods must lead to a collapse of the mark. [18]

Although the gist of the Treasury briefing was still on the old lines of budgetary orthodoxy at the national level there was recognition that economic expansion actually eased the problems of government finance. Following the protection of the home market by tariffs in 1931, a general rise in economic activity had increased government revenues and prosperity *without* any massive increase in overseas trade which the Gold Standard enthusiasts would have argued was necessary. *The Times* commented after the April Budget of 1934:

> The nation is entitled to congratulate itself on the fact that, at a time when most foreign countries are suffering from great increasing deficits, the Chancellor of the Exchequer is able to point to a substantial [budgetary] surplus...The improvement reflected in the Budget is due almost entirely to the expansion of the home market and to the greater share in that market secured for home industries. [19]

The improved state of government finances resulting from the underlying recovery in real economic activity at home was to be a recurrent feature of comment in the national press, yet rarely featured in Treasury briefs.

In 1936, the government began a major reappraisal of the state of its defences. Sir Thomas Inskip's appointment as Minister for Co-ordination of Defence was criticized by Churchill, in his general attack on the lackadaisical progress towards effective defence against Germany. Yet it was under Inskip that the deadly grip of Treasury dogma began to ease. Inskip's magnum opus on defence expenditure was sent to Cabinet on 15 December 1937, and the tenor of its economic section shows a significant departure from the normal financial cant:

69

In considering whether we can afford this or that programme, the first question asked is how much the programme will cost; and the cost of the programme is then related to the sums which can be made available from Exchequer resources, from taxation, or exceptionally from the proceeds of loans. But the fact that the problem is considered in terms of money, must not be allowed to obscure the fact that our real resources consist not of money, i.e., paper pounds which are nothing more than a symbol, but of our man power, and productive capacity, our power to maintain our credit, and the general balance of our trade. [20]

It was clear that the die-hards of financial orthodoxy would argue that the nation could not be defended if it was in financial ruin, and that financial ruin might well come if budgets were not balanced and so on. Inskip carefully pointed out that, although financial stability was important:

The whole trend of modern armaments is in the direction of reliance on mechanised forces, capable of dealing a knockout blow in a few weeks or months. If our superior staying power is to be brought to bear to bring us victory in war, we must maintain forces strong enough to ensure us against defeat by a sudden blow. [21]

In this way, Inskip was ready for the Treasury inspired argument that sound finance would be a better defence than say, a few more squadrons of Spitfires. There were those in Cabinet ready to defend the old Treasury faith, however. Chamberlain's five years as a very orthodox Chancellor had left their impression strongly upon him. Furthermore, there were keen appeasers and orthodox finance men in the highest positions in his Cabinet. It is difficult to disentangle whether fear of financial disorganization, following orthodox Treasury thinking, led ministers to desire appeasement, or whether desire for appeasement led them to use orthodox financial arguments as a rationalization.

By 16 February 1938, Inskip had re-modelled his package to represent a comprehensive defensive scheme costing a maximum of £1650 million over the five years 1937-1941. The response of Sir John Simon, the Chancellor of the Exchequer, was that: 'He wished to place on record however, that the expenditure of £1650 million on defence not only placed a terrible strain on the national finances but could not be increased without financial disorganisation to an extent that would weaken the resistance of the country.'[22]

Lord Halifax, who at the end of 1937 had encountered 'friendliness and a desire for good relations'[23] during his informal visit to Hitler, supported the Treasury line in Cabinet that day: 'He felt also that it was very difficult for any member of the Cabinet to ignore the Chancellor of the Exchequer's grave warning – as grave, perhaps, as any Chancellor had ever uttered – as to the danger of exceeding these figures.'[24] Chamberlain took the orthodox logic a little further at the Emergency Cabinet three days later:

> Our own credit position was an immense strength to the country and in itself was a strong deterrent to war unless an aggressor felt that he could knock us out in the early stages of a war. Consequently we could not get away from that position unless we contemplated some arrangement which would include a reduction or limitation of armaments within a reasonable time. He had felt, therefore, grave apprehensions not only owing to the growing risks of war but also on the score of financial stringency, and had thought it necessary to consider whether he could make a last effort to alleviate the situation, either by some concessions to Germany or some lightening of the position vis-à-vis Italy.[25]

Thus Chamberlain was using the orthodox financial argument as a compelling reason to seek appeasement of Germany and Italy, since it would seem that he felt that even defence against the knock-out blow might be beyond the nation's means.

It was agreed amongst Cabinet, and insisted upon by Inskip, that the key to defence of the UK was to be the Royal Air Force. Inskip was particularly anxious that most emphasis in the air force programme should go to fighter aircraft rather than bombers. This had also been the thrust of Churchill's argument for some five years. Gross expenditure on the RAF rose from £50 million in 1937 to £133.8 million in 1939. [26] The Treasury had continued to oppose expansion of the RAF first-line strength as late as April 1938, when the Air Minister, Viscount Swinton, commended 'Scheme L' for the RAF to Cabinet, as being essential to meet the menace of German air strength.[27] In the event, Britain's air strength proved to be adequate by a razor-thin margin. But in the years leading up to 1937, the lack of preparedness had been a national scandal and the economic advice given to ministers relentlessly perverse.

It is worth noting that while the Treasury appeared to be constantly repining the lack of financial resources, the real economy was actually generating an output massively higher than that which had been reached during the brief golden age from 1925 to 1929. The chart on page 57 shows clearly the way that industrial production reached a level 30% higher than the previous pre-crash peak in 1937. Throughout the period from 1932 to 1938, national income in both real and nominal terms had been rising at a significant pace: off the Gold Standard, and behind protective trade barriers. Government spending had been falling steadily as a percentage of national income. In 1932, Civil government expenditure had been 21.9% of net national income. By 1938, it was 20.4%. The absolute horror of extra taxation is difficult to comprehend. The standard tax rate in the pound was 5 shillings (25p) in 1932, and a little below this up until 1938 when it was put up to 5 shillings once again.

Yet in a 'think paper', produced at the Treasury in 1936, the picture of imminent catastrophe as a result of high defence expenditure was colourfully painted. The paper, entitled Financing the Defence Programme, contained many cherished Treasury beliefs:

> On a longer view into the more distant future it is hard to see how, taking good times with bad, we can finance our present level of expenditure (unless the cost of armaments goes down to the old level) without a substantial expansion in the money income of the community as a whole. Unless this can be secured higher taxation of the highest incomes seems almost impossible and the question will become one of laying substantially heavier burdens on the population at large if in fact the population can be persuaded or compelled to stand it. [28]

Inherent in the Treasury's thinking was the basic assumption that the economy was static. Any attempt at increasing economic activity was as self-defeating as an attempt to lift yourself by your own bootlaces. Germany, which had obviously transgressed the rules of economic decency by a large margin, was at first forecast to suffer a humiliating financial crash. When total disaster did not come, it was ignored, from the financial analysis point of view. The expansion in the money income mentioned above was thus seen to be synonymous with inflation and eventual ruin.

It is interesting that as the 'real' world problems of an aggressive group of possible enemies grew, the thinking of Cabinet tended to be gradually more focused on *real* economic resources rather than the technicality of financial resources. Inskip's paper clearly emphasized this point. Even Chamberlain began talking of the problems of shortages of skilled labour for armaments work in early 1938, although this sudden appreciation of the real world formed part of his general opposition to the implications of the Inskip proposals. No one attempted to learn anything from the economic events on the continent. As Duff Cooper commented:

> The Treasury, like a governess foretelling the awful fate that is bound to overtake other children who enjoy liberties that are denied to her own charges, has been telling us for years that these naughty, reckless countries will soon go bankrupt. But they don't. They seem to thrive on their folly and batten upon their own extravagance. [29]

By 1938 the Treasury did have a more remarkable explanation for the failure of bankruptcy to overtake the German spendthrifts: this was that the rearmament widely reported was not actually taking place! Lord Balogh has written on this issue:

> In 1938 an estimate I made of the Nazi rearmament (which turned out on the basis of the data captured at the end of the war to be some 25 per cent too low) was said by the two Treasury experts in charge of German economic intelligence to be about 100 per cent too high. Yet even after May 1940 no effect was made to rectify the method of estimate. [30]

Lord Balogh recalls that he was invited into the Treasury after making his estimates to hear from the Treasury experts why it was *theoretically* impossible for the Germans to have been spending the amount on armaments which he had estimated – so the governess finally explained that there was no awful fate for the reckless countries, because they had not actually been reckless.

Some authors have sought to excuse the Treasury's resistance to rearmament on the grounds that the Treasury advice was framed within a genuine assessment of industrial potential. But there is no evidence that the Treasury ever seriously thought about the meaning or implications of industrial capacity. Even an author such as G.C. Peden, who has tried to argue that Chamberlain, Fisher and

Hopkins exercised a 'considerable and constructive influence' on defence policy has noted that:

> There can be little doubt that advisers at the Treasury, even Fisher, who was an advocate of rearmament from 1933, must share heavy responsibility for retrenchment at the expense of defence down to that year (1932). The rigid financial orthodoxy of the Treasury in the Nineteen-Twenties and early Nineteen-Thirties set tight limits to government expenditure, and in the Nineteen-Twenties Fisher shared the prevailing optimism about the international environment.[31]

All the evidence examined in this chapter suggests, however, that the 'rigid financial orthodoxy' continued its baneful influence right up to the last moment. The priorities eventually given the RAF were the product of Inskip's work, and pressure outside government, not least the campaign mounted by Winston Churchill. The chart on page 75 shows graphically the smallness of the concession to rearmament finally made in the late 1934s. The Treasury richly deserved the obscurity which it found in wartime when Churchill became Prime Minister.

The reluctance to think about the economy in any terms but the static survived the Keynesian revolution in one important way – this was the resistance to resource planning. Keynes's idea that the level of economic output was a variable, partly under the control of the state through public expenditure, had been borne out by events of the 1930s, and Keynes's views became widely accepted across the political spectrum. The White Paper produced in 1944, entitled 'Employment Policy' began with the words: 'The Government accept as one of their primary aims and responsibilities the maintenance of a high and stable level of employment after the war.' This marked the eclipse of the hallowed ideas on finance and economic purpose that had been the Treasury's main spiritual sustenance for two decades up to the Second World War. As an eminent Treasury historian has noted: 'From 1939 until 1942 the Treasury was under a political shadow which not only diminished its customary prestige and authority but disqualified it from access to the new centres of deliberation.'[32]

The real planning of the economy for a war footing was carried on largely outside the Treasury by new departments. The Treasury's temporary demotion was well marked on the arrival of Churchill as

# Table 6: *Government expenditure, 1920–39*[33]

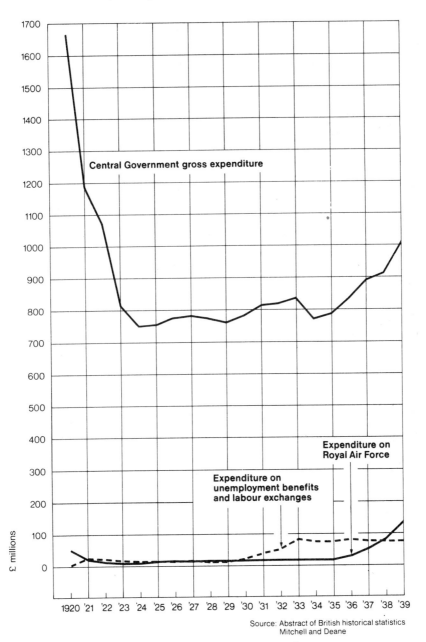

Central Government gross expenditure

Expenditure on
Royal Air Force

Expenditure on
unemployment benefits
and labour exchanges

£ millions

1920 '21 '22 '23 '24 '25 '26 '27 '28 '29 '30 '31 '32 '33 '34 '35 '36 '37 '38 '39

Source: Abstract of British historical statistics
Mitchell and Deane

Prime Minister with the removal of the Chancellor of the Exchequer from the War Cabinet. Paradoxically, the beginning of the Treasury's rehabilitation coincided with the arrival in its midst of Keynes, the erstwhile opponent, as a special wartime adviser. Besides advising on financial aspects of the wartime economy, Keynes was to play the leading role for Britain in the restructuring of the international system of payments which was formalized in the 1944 Bretton Woods agreement. Keynes was far from being a political radical, however, and his influential views and practical activities were not particularly in tune with the economic intentions of the post-war Labour government.

> It is not the ownership of the instruments of production which it is important for the State to assume. If the State is able to determine the aggregate amount of resources devoted to augmenting the instruments and the basic rate of reward to those who own them, it will have accomplished all that is necessary. Moreover, the necessary measures of socialisation can be introduced gradually and without a break in the general traditions of society.[34]

In 1945, the Labour Cabinet set out to prepare the scene for active government intervention on the economic front for a five-year period. At one of the first Cabinet meetings:

> It was pointed out that, apart from the possibility that the House of Lords would be unwilling to renew these powers [economic controls] in two years' time, it was important that the Government should at once establish the principle that the next five years would be a period of transition in which the exercise of emergency powers by the Executive would be as necessary as it had been in War. It was also pointed out that after the last war the period of industrial and economic difficulty had not begun until 1921; and it was arguable that, if the Government had enjoyed sufficient powers of economic control, it would have been possible to avoid the crises of 1921, 1924 and 1926.[35]

The unnecessary misery of the 1920s and 1930s was deeply felt by the whole of the Labour movement, and the reaction against *laissez-faire* policies was fundamental. It was, moreover, well remembered that a Labour government had destroyed itself by adhering to such orthodoxy in 1931.

But there was no desire to enter into authoritarian planning amongst even the most interventionist of the Labour ministers with economic responsibilities. In September, 1945, Stafford Cripps commented in Cabinet that: 'We should avoid the impression that we wish to impose upon industry a preconceived Government plan.'[36] This was most sensible, since in any event, there was no such plan in existence. The first steps to move in the planning direction were put forward in his proposals for 'Industrial Organisation and Efficiency':

> The main feature of his scheme was that there should be an investigation into each industry with the primary object of ascertaining and agreeing with both sides of industry what the industry needed in order to make it as efficient as possible in the national interest. Each investigation would be conducted by a committee consisting as to one third of the employers' representatives, one third of Trade Unionists, and one third of people appointed by himself, including a chairman of high standing.[37]

This rather permissive approach to the groundwork of plans was to apply to the pottery, wool, footwear and furniture industries, and the preparation of efficiency schemes by the Board of Trade was to follow the committee work.

Before the end of 1945, the Chancellor of the Exchequer, Hugh Dalton, introduced a proposal to Cabinet to set up a National Investment Council:

> This Council would include the Governor of the Bank of England, the Chairman of the Capital Issues Committee and the Public Works Loans Board and a number of other persons chosen for their knowledge and experience of financial, economic and industrial questions. Its functions would be advisory and not executive. In this respect it would differ from the National Investment Board which had for long formed part of the Labour Party Programme; but the situation was different now that a Government was in power which was ready itself to take positive action to plan the use of the nation's economic resources. In present circumstances executive functions with regard to the control of investment should be exercised by the Government itself.[38]

It would have been a most naive Cabinet minister who did not recognize the Treasury's 'old favourites' regrouping, with a Labour Chancellor's backing. After all, the Cunliffe Committee of 1924 had been set up by a Labour Chancellor, with an ex-Conservative Chancellor as its chairman (see page 47), and had supported narrow financial interests. In 1945, the Chancellor was asked by his colleagues to make it clear publicly that any such council would form 'only part of wider proposals for economic planning'.[39]

Nearly thirty years later, yet another Labour Chancellor set up a rival source of funds, the Lever Bank – set apart from the Labour Party's promised National Enterprise Board...*plus ça change*. The political motivation was much the same, whether it was partly regarded as camouflage for the benefit of foreigners, or more honestly as a way of diluting and diverting political purpose.

It was nevertheless to take several years before the Treasury resumed its unchallenged position as economic policy-maker and before ministers like Harold Wilson found prominence and popularity with a 'bonfire of controls'. As late as 1947, it was still the Prime Minister who introduced the draft White Paper on the Economic Survey in Cabinet. The crises which deflected the Labour government from further serious attempts at planning in more than an *ad hoc* fashion were many. In 1947, for instance, they had to think of ways of producing more coal. The foreign exchange crises are described elsewhere. The Cabinet ministers appear to have liked the idea of economic planning, but not to have known how to develop a system to carry out their wishes. As the Treasury became more influential, and indeed took on board the department with the grand title of 'Central Economic Planning Staff' so the actuality of planning dissolved. The lack of a sense of direction felt by civil servants at the time is illustrated by the following.

As part of the Marshall Aid programme, the recipients of assistance from the US were obliged to submit fairly detailed 'long-term' plans to the newly formed Organization for European Economic Co-operation. The plans were to show how the nations intended to restore output and potential to levels sufficient to allow them to attain stability in the pattern of their trade balances within a period of four years from 1948. Britain's submission was described as 'no more and no less than a statement of economic strategy' – and it was an ambitious and detailed document which J. C. R. Dow believed 'dominated policy during the next few years'.[40] The information now available at the Public Records Office does not seem to illustrate this kind of conviction on the part of the civil servants involved.

On 27 October 1948, Austin Robinson wrote from the British Delegation at the OEEC in Paris to Robert Hall, then head of the Economic Section at the Cabinet Office:

> My own difficulty here is that I do not know whether or not HMG has any thought out policy for giving effect to the figures which somewhat light-heartedly are being written into programmes...
>
> The Spierenburg paper which we discussed yesterday was from our point of view alarming, because it sought to put the liberalisation of international trade right in the forefront. Here we are finding it quite extraordinarily difficult to know how far to resist that type of approach, because we do not know what you others have been thinking and assuming in this field. I myself have always assumed that it was our idea to move rather slowly from the controlled economy in Europe to the liberal economy in Europe, and that during the process of transition we would look to the use of controls...as a means of making the trades flow.[41]

On 1 November, Robert Hall wrote: 'I spoke to Austin this morning and told him that I did not think anyone in London knew the answer; but that I would consult you [Rowan].'[42] A few days later on the same issue, Sir Sidney Caine at the Treasury commented: 'In the main it seems to me that our programmes are nearer to estimates than intentions. We shall do what we can to make them come true but we do not intend to dragoon everybody else into complying with them.'[43]

The lack of clear objectives from 1945 to 1951 seemed to Monnet to be a key fault in the development of British economic policy. With the planning he instituted, a major initial objective was to obtain a joint view on targets between all sides represented, trade-unionists, industrialists, and civil servants. Most important was to act on the French plans with the minimum of delay.

> The idea of a plan belonged to the realm of ideological controversy over the Soviet Five-year plan; and I knew that only action could dissipate misunderstandings about the entirely new type of planning that we had in mind.

This was as far removed from the Soviet *Gosplan* or State Planning Commission as it was from the unique system that Sir Stafford Cripps, the British Chancellor of the Exchequer, had established to organize a concerted national effort on the part of the United Kingdom. We had studied the operation of Cripps' 'working parties', which brought together industrialists, trade unionists, and technical experts, but this democratic attempt to steer the economy seemed to us seriously handicapped by the absence of civil servants representing the public interest, as well as by its lack of general objectives. Improving upon this precedent, we quickly hit upon what seemed the right formula, that of our 'Modernization Commissions'.[44]

There was no mistaking the nationalistic and purposeful tone of Monnet's first note to de Gaulle on the modernization and investment plan for France. Over the personnel for his planning office, Monnet had few illusions about the likely enthusiasm of long-serving bureaucrats:

'I have a high regard for the French civil service,' I said, 'but it is not equipped to produce a plan for changing the face of France. On the contrary, its job is to maintain the state of affairs entrusted to it. The senior civil servants who run it have every quality – except the spirit of enterprise. To transform France, we must first transform the ... French establishment, and perhaps also the training that produces it.'[45]

By contrast, the Labour Cabinet appeared to have no qualms about the commitment of the civil servants whom it entrusted to pursue its policies. Having said that it wanted to plan to use Britain's resources to the full, there seemed to be an assumption that the planning structure would come to be. Only Stafford Cripps put forward concrete proposals for a system that would continue to have a life of its own, as we have seen above. As the orchestrated campaign against its principles and policies got under way, and with Cripps moved to the Treasury, a focus for the development of purposes and means disappeared.

It is clear that the sense of a common objective which the French obtained between different sides of industry was never established by the Labour government. The bitter attacks and vigorous propaganda launched against the Labour government's policies by the Federation of British Industries and sectors of the press gave them little chance. Towards the end of 1947, Attlee remarked in a speech: 'We have got to get something other than the profit motive. I cannot see why the motive of service to the community should not operate in peace as it did in war.'[46]

A *Financial Times* editorial on 1 September attacked him sharply, with the argument that Labour's appeals to national unity and purpose were not appropriate in peacetime. Wartime analogies were not appropriate to the realities of commerce. But by this time, the Labour government had lost its opportunity to establish objectives and a common ground for modernization and improvement in the French style.

As Chancellor, Cripps certainly carried over to the Treasury certain heretical views on economic purpose. J. C. R. Dow has commented: 'At times, he almost appeared to regard budgetary action as no more than a background to planning proper; too high a level of demand drew off resources to inessential uses, and made "all planning a matter of extreme difficulty".'[47]

Nevertheless, the Labour government attained a large degree of success in many of the economic priorities which it set itself. From 1947 to 1951 Gross Domestic Product rose by 15% – at the same time fixed capital expenditure rose 10%. Investment in manufacturing industry rocketed ahead; the increase from 1948 to 1951 was something like 38% in real terms. This level of investment expansion was to be equalled only once within any three-year span after 1951; and then in conditions of much faster growth in consumer expenditure (1959-61).

Despite rather poor co-ordination of longer-term objectives, the industrial muscle of the British economy developed rapidly under the first post-war Labour government. Steel production managed to grow by nearly a third from 1946 to 1951, coal production by 17%, and electricity generation by over 40%. All of these achievements occurred during a period when the government had been handicapped by coercion by the US to accept disruptive conditions for a large loan, by two major sterling crises, as well as problems posed by the Korean War.

Vicious attacks on the Labour government's attempts to apply industrial priorities and controls were not slow in coming. J. Jewkes, in a study entitled *Ordeal by Planning* wrote: 'Finally, in July 1947, the Government, having learnt and forgotten nothing, announced that the economic crisis called for direction of labour, tighter distribution of raw materials to cut out unessential work, and more elaborate discrimination over capital expansion. In short more of the old poison to cure the disease.'[48]

As G. D. N. Worswick, the distinguished contemporary economic commentator, noted on a graph showing the 40% increase in British industrial production between 1946 and 1950: 'Accustomed as we have become since the war to tales of economic crisis, the chart may come as a shock. Above all, industrial production was rising with extraordinary steadiness at a rate of about 8 per cent per annum throughout the period.'[49] And on the quotation above from Jewkes: 'If the coal distribution breakdown in early 1947 did have any great effect, it can only have been to reduce somewhat the production in 1947, with a consequent exaggeration of the rise in 1948. But that is a very different thing from the picture of an economy shackled by controls and slowly grinding to a stop.'[50]

The system was very far from being perfect. But it did allow the most remarkable five years of industrial growth that have been seen in post-war Britain. It might have been thought that the ghosts of pre-war doctrine had been laid. But as we shall see in the next chapter, the change of government in 1951 brought with it a sharp shift away from planning, that eventually led to a complete departure from all that had apparently been learnt from Keynes. The drift away from Keynesian economic management was to induce an almost complete stagnation of the economy by the late 1970s.

REFERENCES

1  *Evening Standard*, 26 October 1938
2  *The Times*, 26 February 1938
3  Shay, Robert Paul, *British Rearmament in the Thirties*, Princeton University Press 1977, p. 282
4  CAB 27/115, 23 September 1920
5  CAB 27/119, 26 September 1921
6  ibid.
7  ibid.
8  Mitchell, B. R. and Deane, P., *Abstract of British Historical Statistics*, Cambridge University Press 1962, p. 345
9  T177/25, 27 November 1936, draft briefing note from F. Phillips, Treasury Under Secretary, to Sir Richard Hopkins amongst

     notes attached to 'Financing the Defence Programme'
10   ibid.
11   T176/5, 8 June 1921, note from Sir B. Blackett to Chancellor
     of the Exchequer
12   LAB 2/1361, 22 March 1921
13   Swann, Brenda and Turnbull, Maureen, *Records of Interest to
     Social Scientists 1919 to 1939, Employment and Unemployment*,
     HMSO 1978, p. 13
14   Keynes, John Maynard, *The General Theory of Employment,
     Interest and Money* (first published 1936), Macmillan 1964
15   T208/195, March 1936
16   Cabinet Minutes, 15 February 1933
17   Cabinet Minutes, 25 June 1934
18   T172/1837, 7 March 1935. Note to Warren Fisher by Richard
     Hopkins, 2nd Secretary, on memo from Sir Eric Phipps
19   *The Times*, 18 April 1934
20   CAB 24/273, 15 December 1937
21   ibid.
22   Gilbert, Martin, *Winston S. Churchill*, vol. 5, Heinemann
     1976, p. 888
23   CAB 23/92, 16 February 1938
24   ibid.
25   CAB 23/92, 19 February 1938
26   Mitchell and Deane, op, cit., p. 400
27   Gilbert, op. cit., p. 931
28   T177/25, F. Phillips, see note 9
29   *Evening Standard*, 26 October 1938
30   Balogh, Lord Thomas, 'The Apotheosis of the Dilettante' in
     Thomas, Hugh (ed.), *Crisis in the Civil Service*, Anthony
     Blond 1968, p. 17
31   Peden, G.C. *British Rearmament and the Treasury 1932– 39*,
     Scottish Academic Press 1979, p. 7
32   Roseveare, Henry, *The Treasury – The Evolution of a British
     Institution*, Allen Lane 1969, p. 273
33   Mitchell and Deane, op. cit.
34   Keynes, op. cit., p. 378
35   CAB 128, 16 August 1945
36   CP (45) 142. Paper by Stafford Cripps, President of the Board
     of Trade
37   CAB 128, September 1945
38   CAB 128, Cabinet Minutes, 22 November 1945

39  CAB 128, 22 November 1945
40  Dow, J. C. R., *The Management of the British Economy 1945-60*, Cambridge University Press 1964, NIESR, p. 31
41  T230/109, 27 October 1948
42  T230/109, 1 November 1948
43  T230/109, 9 November 1948
44  Monnet, Jean, *Memoirs* (trans. R. Mayne), Collins 1978, p. 237
45  Monnet, op. cit., p. 245
46  *Financial Times*, 1 September 1947
47  Dow, op. cit., p. 36
48  Jewkes, J., 'Ordeal by Planning' quoted in Worswick, G.D.N., *The British Economy 1945–1950*, Oxford University Press 1952, p. 6
49  ibid.
50  ibid.

# 6
# Post-War Decline – 1951 Onwards

*The traditional Tory attitude to Civil Servants has been one of lordly disdain; one leading Conservative politician still refers to them as 'clerks'. On the other hand policy under Conservative rule seems to have originated largely from Civil Servants. I do not mean that official advice has always been taken – far from it – but that ministers have relied on Civil Servants to provide the intellectual framework on which decisions are ultimately based.*

*An extraordinary feature of Conservative economic performance is that it grew worse rather than better as time went on.*
*Samuel Brittan,* The Treasury under the Tories 1951–1964, *1964*[1]

Did the incoming Conservative government of 1951 show clear signs of economic purpose? Did it have a new direction for the economy that it would use the Civil Service machine to steer? The answer to both these questions is basically 'no'. Under the Conservatives, the government tended to follow the 'reformed' Keynesian Treasury line. But as Treasury influence grew more pervasive some of the 'old' Treasury rules once more began to find favour.

We have noted in Chapter 5 that the virtual disappearance of Treasury influence during the Second World War was accompanied by a most successful re-organization of the nation's industrial resources. The existence of this system of controls and administrative machinery certainly helped the incoming Labour government with its own economic management. The austerity which accompanied post-war revival was not popular – although many aspects of the policy were successful in rebuilding an industrial base for peacetime needs. But the Labour Cabinet tended to shrink back from a continued whole-hearted commitment to planning, and there was no lack of news coverage for any shortcomings in the existing system.

The long run trends in relative economic growth began to turn against Britain after 1951. The Treasury had regained much of its old influence under Stafford Cripps, but its style remained for some years heavily influenced by the experience of wartime and the immediate post-war years. It was 1958 before the Treasury's planning department was dissolved, for example.

Britain's decline, and the scale of its magnitude, was first noticed under the Macmillan administration, and it seems that the drive to join the apparently successful European Common Market was the fruit of an ideological interpretation of Britain's malaise. It was felt that the Common Market nations were successful because somehow trade was freer the other side of the Channel. If Britain could also enjoy the bracing tonic of enhanced competition, everything would be resolved. More particularly, prospects would be improved with no extra effort from government. This was a fundamental return in thinking to the pre-war Treasury view that free trade and the Gold Standard would bring prosperity. Such a euphoric view of the process of European growth could only be entertained in ignorance of the facts of French planning, and with little attention to the purposefully structured German financial and industrial machine.

So the 'ideological' rather than pragmatic attachment to 'free market forces' was no new thing. Furthermore, certain members of Labour's post-war administration gloried in the 'bonfire of controls', and welcomed the move towards market liberalization. Considering the lesson the 1930s taught of the advantages of not being 'free markets', this is particularly surprising. The passive acceptance of the trend by Labour activists was also a puzzling feature of this episode.

Reaction against the fruits of Macmillan's style of 'Keynesian' *laissez-faire* and a wider view of Britain's problems was demonstrated by the Labour Party's 'Twelve Wasted Years', one of the most interesting election campaign documents issued in the last few decades.[2] 'Twelve Wasted Years' illustrated clearly the speed with which Britain had declined against other countries from 1951 to 1963 – a period which was being sold to the general public as a period of extraordinary prosperity, which could be repeated, the public was told, by continued freedom of market forces although presumably forces not quite as bracing as would have been available inside the Common Market. Private Consumption Expenditure did indeed rise by some 46% in the period of Conservative government. Considerable assistance to this rise in prosperity had been afforded by the relative cheapness of raw materials, compared with the prices of manufactures, which Britain still produced effectively. However, the lead over the European industrial countries in providing machinery and vehicles for the rest of the world was being eroded fast, and little thought had been directed by the upper echelons of administration to methods of ensuring a prosperous national future, other than by 'freeing the market' on an international scale. Treasury rule under the Conservatives had given superficial prosperity, but the underlying indications were grave for the economy.

The increasingly worrying performance of the economy under the Conservatives from 1951 to 1963 was put in the shade by developments under the economically timorous administration of Harold Wilson from 1964 to 1970. The mistakes of the Conservatives with 'stop-go' reactions to sterling crises were magnified. Brave words were spoken in the run-up to the 1964 election, and bold statements on economic policy were aired:

> The Labour Party has always argued that an economy based on free market principles was bound to fail. For the last twelve years the economic prosperity of the nation has depended on uncoordinated decisions taken by managers of a few hundred large firms. Decisions which do not add up to an economic plan for growth. Under a Labour government planning machinery will be developed so that there will be close and continuing co-operation between industry and Government in the achievement of planning goals.[3]

Nevertheless, the Labour administration of the 1960s allowed its attention to be focused on the endemic weakness of Britain's balance of payments throughout its period of office, enduring the agony of the 1967 devaluation, and the deflationary policies introduced by Roy Jenkins. It had become clear that Labour administrations would tend to keep growth low rather than risk the possible humiliations of further devaluations – which they had convinced themselves were admissions of defeat, rather than strategic stances offering fresh possibilities. One aggressive strategy in 1964 would have been a quick devaluation shortly after coming into office, before the speculators began to be really active against sterling. Yet it is clear that the Labour Prime Minister, Harold Wilson, had set his mind against this type of approach before his premiership. He wrote in his account of that conjuncture:

> There was comment, and this has been subsequently echoed, that we made an initial, even fatal, blunder in our decision not to devalue within twenty four hours of taking office, when we could have put all the responsibility on our Conservative predecessors. Politically, it might have been tempting and we were not unaware of the temptation. But I was convinced, and my colleagues agreed, that to devalue could have the most dangerous consequences.[4]

The 'dangerous consequences' mentioned by Wilson in his account were in fact rather unconvincing. Basically they were that devaluation would lead to a mental association between Labour governments and devaluation, leading to endless speculative scares – that a British devaluation would require 'brutal restraints in both public and private expenditure' in order to allow resources to be transferred to the foreign sector. Controls on imports by quota were rejected by the Labour administration. According to Harold Wilson: 'I had had enough experience of administering them in the forties to know the damage they could inflict on industrial production.'[5]

In fact, the net result of Labour's policy paralysis over the foreign account problems was that demand was held back to such an extent that industrial production only increased at an average of 2½ % each year from 1964 to 1970. The Conservatives had achieved just over 3% each year, on average, from 1951 to 1964, even with their 'stop-go' problems. The average annual growth in Maudling's 'dash for growth' had been nearly 6% in the two years up to the end of 1964 and the election.

The fiasco of the 1967 sterling crisis killed that major institutional symbol of longer-term economic thinking by the 1964–70 Labour government, the Department of Economic Affairs. The spring budget of 1968 was described by Harold Wilson as 'the most punishing budget in Britain's peacetime history' – but this comment is a little misleading, to the extent that private consumption, having fallen back slightly, managed to rebound after the budget by 2% from the second quarter of 1968 to the same period the following year. Nevertheless, the measure was well in the tradition of 1950s 'stop-go'. Consumer spending was less damaged than manufacturing industry.

Industrial production in 1970 was only 1% higher than it had been the year before, and the 2% growth in Gross Domestic Product came largely from consumer spending. Despite the evident stagnation of the economy, a further cautious budget was introduced in 1970 – leaving industrial production stagnating into 1971, and weak, consumer-led growth of Gross Domestic Product. This was a more profound legacy for the incoming Conservative government than the vaunted balance of payments surplus. Jenkins was nevertheless hailed as some kind of economic wonder; a highly questionable view considering the industrial statistics of the 1940s.

Over the period 1964–1970, British industrial production increased by 15.7% compared with 38.9% in France and 41.6% in Germany. Britain had grown under Wilson at less than half the rate achieved by her main European rivals.

The Conservative administration of 1970–74, short though it was, proved to be highly significant. One aspect was that it demonstrated the increased awareness of Britain's backwardness that gripped British politicians even after entry to the administrative mausoleum of Whitehall. Edward Heath was very different from Harold Wilson most importantly in that he firmly believed that the function of government was to achieve national and economic purposes. Furthermore, Heath was more clearly exercised by the progressive decline of the UK than Wilson had been. The trial of harsh economic policies, the 'Selsdon' experiment, was shortlived – possibly because of a lack of 'Selsdon Men' in the corps of British management – and rather unorthodox growth policies were introduced. The main element of unorthodoxy was the 'floating' of the pound – a measure that was more imaginative than any economic decision since 1951. There was a measure of difficulty on the inflation front, where the RPI exceeded 9% by 1973. Nevertheless, industry was given an impetus it had not experienced for years. In the period 1970–73 British industrial output increased 12%. French output increased by 23.8%, and German output by 13%. So Britain still lagged, but by a smaller margin than before.

'*Laissez-faire*', which might be interpreted in the British usage as 'let it happen', rather than 'let it be done' – had a rather short life under Heath. The 'hidden hand' of free market forces was not going to deliver the goods in time for his satisfaction – and this seems a more traditional Tory reaction, containing a laudable pragmatism. Unfortunately, part of Heath's way of speeding things up involved a tough pay policy. He had lost patience with dilatory British management, who had failed to respond to the demand stimulus that Heath had boldly delivered to the economy. What evidence is available about the events leading up to the three-day week docs seem to suggest that Heath was encouraged to take on the unions by Civil Service mandarins – who apparently preferred to blame the unions for British economic failure than to suggest any imperfection in their own historic blend of deflation and *laissez-faire*.

Before moving on to the dramatic events following the oil crisis of December 1973, it is worth considering some salient features of the period of 'benevolent' Treasury rule during the 1950s and 1960s.

One striking aspect of the economy was persistently low relative domestic investment. The relationship between low investment and low growth in output is not at all straightforward. It is both true that a lack of investment inhibits healthy increases in output at times of high demand and that investment will not occur at times when equipment is under-utilized. So low growth tends to generate low growth in investment, and low investment limits the potential for growth. It is unnecessary to ask, 'which came first?' Having seen the relative industrial growth and income growth levels for the UK we should not be surprised at figures showing the relative investment impoverishment of the British manufacturer. It was evident in the early 1950s that British investment per head was lagging behind that of other European nations – despite the fact that they were at the time considerably less rich on a per capita basis. The following table shows figures derived from the *Economic Survey of Europe*, published in 1958.

Table 7:  *Average annual investment per employee in 1953 at 1954 prices*[6]

| | |
|---|---|
| W. Germany | $650 |
| Italy | $620 |
| UK | $400 |
| France | $590 |

1953 was a reasonably good year for British investment. By the late 1950s the UK was still investing a much lower proportion of its national income than its major European rivals – and this trend continued into the 1960s and beyond as the following table shows.

Table 8:  *Investment as a percentage of GNP (manufacturing sector)*[7]

| | 1950–59 | 1960–69 |
|---|---|---|
| W.Germany | 17.8 | 18.8 |
| Italy | 21.4 | 18.1 |
| France | 18.2 | 23.9 |
| UK | 12.1 | 13.0 |

These poor performances were continued year by year into the 1970s. The new Chancellor of the 1974–79 Labour administration commented:

For each worker in industry British firms have been investing only two-thirds as much as German firms, only one-third as much as French firms, and under a quarter as much as Japanese firms. The result is not just that these countries have raced ahead of us in output. It means that industrial wages in Britain are now lower than they are in Japan.[8]

Whether it was the low growth which led to low investment, or vice versa, it is clear from all these figures that investment in Britain has not been taking place on a scale likely to enable rapid technical progress and innovation in the way it was possible in many other countries. So one link in the 'vicious circle' was well forged, as we have seen, at the beginning of the 1950s.

Even in the great pinnacle of investment in 1970, of which Labour politicians became so proud in later and lesser years, British investment lagged lamentably behind that of other comparable nations.

Table 9:   *Gross physical investment, all sectors, per head of population, 1970*[9]

|  | £ |
| --- | --- |
| UK | 172 |
| France | 356 |
| W.Germany | 371 |
| Holland | 279 |
| Belgium | 269 |
| Italy | 164 |

The level of investment in manufacturing industry reached by the United Kingdom in 1970 was not exceeded over the following nine years.

From 1945 the predominant characteristic of government economic management was its instability, closely related to sterling's unduly exposed position to speculation. Yet, two governments seemed to sustain certain underlying economic objectives despite the 'Achilles' heel' of the pound. These were the first Labour government 1945–51, and Heath's Conservative government 1970–73. External circumstances were difficult for both these governments, yet they managed to maintain objectives for what can be described as sustained periods. Mr Maudling's dash for growth was never really tested. Mr Heath's economic policy came to grief on two counts – the confrontation with the miners and the oil crisis. Throughout the whole period, government policy has seemed to revolve through phases of stimulation without pay policy, crisis followed by either deflation or tough policies on pay or both. Following hard on these phases came a period of stagnation, with protest growing against unemployment and increased awareness of Britain's declining position. No other major power went through such policy convulsions, and no other nation economically comparable with Britain in the 1950s had such a poor record of economic growth, industrial production and poor export performance.

## Table 10: *Manufacturing output, UK and other European countries*[10]

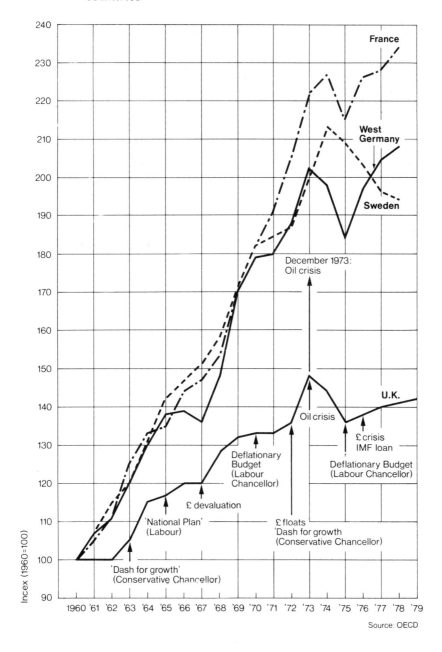

Source: OECD

The decline from 1955 was fairly steady under both Conservative and Labour administrations. Examination of the historical record shows a remarkable pattern of repetition – and what could be described as a failure to learn anything from the previous cycles of experience. Nothing seemed to have been learned by the British political and civil administration, either from Britain's own experience, or from the experience of similar industrial countries enduring the same world economic climate. The chart on page 93 shows the graphic decline of Britain as a manufacturing power in Europe. Meanwhile confidence in Keynesian management was gradually declining. The administration always seemed to be completely surprised by the scale of speculation against sterling, and always unable to do anything other than cut growth, or devalue, or both to satisfy speculative opinion. Yet the speculative movements themselves have frequently been independent of the actual state of the British economy – related sometimes to events in other currencies, or to movements of foreign interest rates. Yet clearly a powerful lobby inside the UK favoured this state of affairs and has been able to dissuade effective measures being taken to limit sterling's world role, up to Barber's flotation of sterling in 1972.

The phenomenon of chronic unreadiness on the foreign balance side was to become more marked under the Labour government 1974–79, and this is the central feature of the following chapter. Paradoxically, it was to be under this Labour government that the interests of finance were to be served far ahead of industry, reversing Heath's priorities. Once more, the old Treasury rules, those of the 1920s, were to be given full rein.

REFERENCES

1  Brittan, Samuel, *The Treasury under the Tories 1951–1964*, Penguin 1964, p. 162
2  'Twelve Wasted Years' published by the Labour Party, 1963
3  op. cit., p. 101
4  Wilson, Harold, *The Labour Government 1964–70*, 1971, reprinted Pelican 1974, p. 27
5  Wilson, op. cit., p. 28

6   Economic Council for Europe
7   OECD National Accounts quoted in Samuels, J. M. and Goddard, C. S., *Company Finance in Europe*, The Institute of Chartered Accountants 1975, p. 326
8   Denis Healey, speaking to the Parliamentary Labour Party, Labour Party Press Release, 25 February 1976
9   OECD financial statistics quoted in Samuels and Goddard, op. cit., p. 4
10  OECD, industrial production statistics

# 7

# To the Watershed of 1976

*I don't have powerful intellectual convictions about the way the economy operates. I have developed my position very much by trial and error.*

*Denis Healey, 1979*[1]

The previous chapter noted the breathtaking scale of Britain's relative decline from 1951 to 1970. However, the chart on page 93 also records the way in which the new Conservative Chancellor's expansionist policies brought about a substantial revival in Britain's position from 1971 to 1973. It is important to realize that this was an increase in 'real' goods produced inside Britain by manufacturing industry, not the windfall gains from the North Sea, nor a transitory monetary phenomenon. It was not, in itself, an expansion based upon 'living beyond our means'–the 'means' themselves expanded. As the means expanded from 1971 to 1973, so unemployment fell dramatically, as can be seen in table 11. As Churchill had surmised some fifty years before, the reduction of unemployment meant the generation of extra resources.

The first subject of the present chapter is the crisis which followed upon the heels of the 'Barber boom'. This related to the world situation rather than to the aftermath of Conservative policies. The collision between the Conservative government and the National Union of Mineworkers at the end of 1973 provided a background for an election in 1974 which Labour narrowly won, albeit with no workable majority. The government formed in March had only five more seats than the Conservative opposition, and there were thirty-seven seats held by Liberals and other parties. Thus a confused economic situation was overlaid with considerable political instability for the new government. The progress from this unpromising start for the economy to deep stagnation and crude monetarism forms the latter part of this chapter. The charts on page 98 indicate the phenomenon familiar from the 1920s–falling output combined with rocketing unemployment. We are unfortunate in having little public access to the arguments which were put forward in Whitehall during this period, since the period from 1974 to 1976 represents a watershed in both economic thinking and policy prescription in post-war Britain. But from various interviews, speeches, signed articles, and from reports of press briefings and 'leaks', the trend can be clearly discerned.

Up to 1974, the benign influence of Keynes was still relatively strong in Treasury counsels, although recurrent anxieties over sterling had biased governments towards dampening growth. Table 12 on page 98 shows the long-run results of this approach. But in the course of the first three years of the new Chancellor's incumbency, the Treasury's thinking reverted to the homilies of the 1920s. It was a sequence of crises and volte-faces of various kinds which brought about this sad degeneration. To be understood, the events must be examined in more detail.

The very first reactions to the oil crisis in 1973 and 1974 were far from panic-stricken. Much advice to government was of the 'wait and see' variety; this was prudent. The economic implications of the crisis were understood early and clearly in the UK; this was to be, paradoxically, dangerous. However, the fact that British policy-makers were well advised on the implications of the oil surplus was to lead them to the belief that all industrial countries would understand the crisis, and that all could be persuaded, or led, to react in an enlightened way. This was a dangerous belief.

The first press reactions in October 1973 tended to give the impression that the increase was a blow, but not a very significant one. This was because the oil price increase was arrived at in several stages over four months. *The Economist* noted: 'For Britain, the higher taxes [on oil] will mean paying an additional £400m a year for oil imports; that is, until North Sea oil begins to flow in earnest.'[2] Already, the scent of future riches for the UK was in the air. However, further oil price increases took place – and the actual

**Table 11:** *Number of persons registered unemployed in the UK (post-war period)*[3]

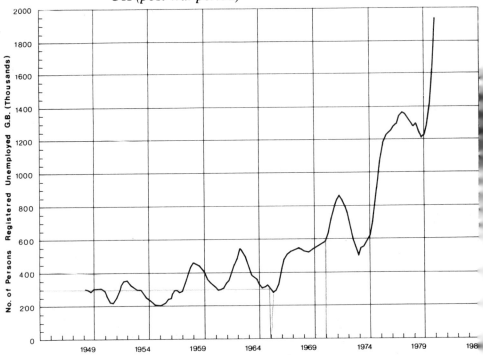

**Table 12:** *Index of industrial production (manufacturing, post-war period)*[4]

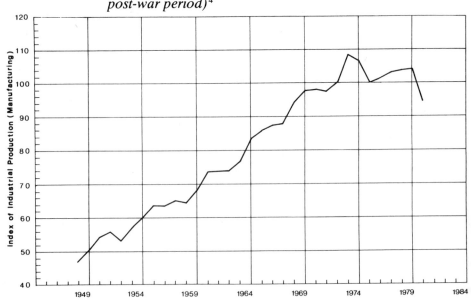

extra cost in 1974 of petroleum imports was £2855 million. This was despite a 6% fall in the tonnage brought in.

The kind of informed advice on world impact that was available at the turn of the year was exemplified by the OECD Secretariat's work. Its calculations, published in December 1973,[5] indicated that the effect of the price increase on the whole OECD area would be $15 billion worth of deflation. When all the price adjustments had been made, the impact would have been over $60 billion worth of recession. The estimate made by the Secretariat for the UK's share of the burden was one-thirtieth of the total; in other words, Britain's domestic energy supplies were anticipated to have an effect of giving Britain a less than proportionate share of the oil burden. Thus, Britain was not perceived as being anything like as exposed in the crisis as, say, Italy or Japan.

By mid-January, however, the full magnitude of the crisis was known. Clear assessments of the future dangers were made–and implications for government policy were set out. In February, the National Institute for Economic and Social Research noted:

> The deflationary hole which the oil price digs in each of the advanced economies can for the time be filled with goods and services for the use of those economies. If it is not, resources released by the oil price rise will remain idle.
>
> It is mainly because of this 'real' deflationary effect that we have revised downwards our forecasts of world production and trade; we do not believe industrial countries will adopt adequate offsetting policies. This initial deflationary impact must, of course, be part of the British Budget calculation.[6]

The Conservative Chancellor, having returned from a meeting of the group of larger industrial countries, the IMF Committee of Twenty, argued that an unorthodox solution to the oil deficit problem would be found: 'By this I mean that, as far as the oil deficits are concerned, there was near unanimity that we should reject the orthodox solution of reliance on domestic deflation associated with external measures such as depreciation of the exchange rate.'[7] The IMF Committee of Twenty had issued a communiqué which stated that the member countries would 'sustain appropriate levels of economic activity and employment'[8] and avoid trade restrictions and competitive devaluation. Exactly what was meant by 'appropriate' was not clearly defined.

The NIESR's February advice to the Chancellor was cautious: 'On balance, a neutral budget might be the best now.'[9] But it was advised that reflationary action should be taken if unemployment continued to mount. The course which the IMF meeting had overtly or apparently turned away from, that of allowing recession to rid a nation of the oil deficit and pass it on to others, was in fact the course to be followed by the big industrial countries other than Britain; but it was some time before this was realized.

The election campaign of spring 1974 took place against the enormous economic uncertainties of both the oil crisis, and the three-day week. This had been introduced as an 'energy saving' emergency measure, which the Conservative government asserted was made necessary by the miners' industrial action. The need for the three-day week was disputed by Labour politicians, and the suspicion existed that it had been a measure taken in order to dramatize the impact on the economy of a large strike. Speaking in Leeds during the election campaign, Denis Healey highlighted the uncertainties that were to overshadow his own first budget:

> By inflicting at least two months of reduced output on British industry, Mr Heath has ruled out the prospect of any growth this year. At the same time we must make room for increased investment and reduce the non-oil deficit in our trade. And, contrary to Mr Barber, Mr Heath says we must export an additional £2,000m of goods to cover the oil deficit as well. This would mean a catastrophic fall in British living standards. It is quite unnecessary and is contrary to the agreements already made in OECD and the IMF.[10]

One of the main attacks made by the Conservatives during the February election campaign was that the Labour programme for action was going to be impossibly expensive. But careful effort had gone in to costing this programme, under the direction of Denis Healey in the Labour Party's Finance and Economic Sub-Committee. A senior official in the Treasury later commented that the document 'Paying for Labour's Programme' was the first serious attempt by a political party in opposition to put realistic numbers to the costs of its potential election pledges. Thus, the future Chancellor could confidently kill two birds with one stone, both refuting accusations of the profligacy of Labour's proposals, and keeping his options open: 'The central problem is not the cost of Labour's programme; it is the collapse of Britain's economy after 3½ years of Mr Barber.'[11]

The theme that Labour would be taking over a terrible economic mess, and that there could be no guarantee of quickly rising standards of living, was emphasized by the Labour leadership throughout the campaign, and indeed the gravity of the economic crisis was echoed by the Liberals. Bad trade figures announced in February focused attention on the consumer-led nature of the Conservatives' boom, and the deficiencies it revealed in British industrial capacity:

> Certainly the deficit is not due as Mr Barber tried to make out yesterday to increased imports of machinery and capital investment...since 1970 imports of television sets have risen 1500%, imports of washing machines have risen 830% and imports of domestic refrigerators have risen by 200%.[12]

A further stick used to beat the Conservative administration at that time was the expansion of the money supply, which had been an automatic by-product of Mr Barber's successful attempts to get the economy moving. An attraction for Labour spokesmen in emphasizing the expansion of the money supply under Mr Barber was that a significant minority of Conservative MPs were also critical of their leadership on this issue. The throw-back to old-fashioned nineteenth-century monetarism had the great attraction that its arguments all sounded very simple, as we have noted in the pages dealing with the 1920s and 1930s. Healey indicated that the new Labour government would be much more interventionist in the face of crisis:

> The scale of the task ahead is formidable indeed. We need a ten per cent increase in manufacturing output to produce a 33% increase in exports of goods if we are to try to close the non-oil deficit and this will mean giving priority to all firms, public or private, which contribute to the export drive, priority in supplies of energy like oil, coal, priority in scarce industrial materials like steel. It can be done, it was done in similar circumstances by the first post-war Labour Government.[13]

When the new government was formed there was no dearth of advice for economic policy.

One document of budget advice that came to the Chancellor in the first two weeks of March was from the Research Department of the Labour Party at Transport House. Since it was a briefing paper, with no special sanction or imprimatur from the party itself, this document, 'The Budget: The Economic Background and Policy Options', received no press coverage.[14] The paper was noteworthy in that it contrasted with internal Treasury documents of the time in setting out a specific period for dealing with the 'non-oil' deficit – in other words, the deficit in the balance of payments due to the adverse trade position before the advent of the oil crisis. The Research Department set out proposals that the aim should be to eliminate the oil deficit over a set number of years as well. Three years were set for the non-oil deficit elimination and five years for halving the oil deficit.

> For Britain, a distinctly slower rate of progress towards elim-
> inating the oil deficit than for other industrial countries may
> be appropriate. The problem of our present heavy non-oil
> deficit (which is not the position of most other industrial
> countries) makes this necessary; while the prospect of our own
> reserves of North Sea Oil coming on stream in the late 1970s
> makes it possible to countenance the consequences of a period
> of prolonged, if diminishing, deficit.[15]

The size of the necessary borrowing abroad was estimated by the Research Department at some £14,300 million – making the assumption that resources were shifted to the balance of payments at about £1¼ billion each year to 1977. Furthermore, growth would be maintained, even if more unorthodox methods of dealing with sterling crises were needed. The possibility was suggested of introducing a two-tier currency system, as had been operated in a number of continental countries over the past decades, and also the possibility of bolstering defences by taking over some of the massive overseas assets of British citizens as needed. Furthermore, it was suggested that import controls might well be needed to deal with the perpetual problem of Britain's chronic trade imbalance. This was the first time that this particular solution had been raised in the context of Britain's crisis at that time.

A further interesting aspect of the document was that it contained the suggestion that tax increases might be introduced later by the Chancellor in response to 'a faster increase in incomes, relative to the rise in prices, than we forecast (for any reason)'. Since the document was also calling for a neutral budget, with a special emphasis on the possible need for extra taxes to keep the public sector Borrowing Requirement down below the feared level of £4,000 million, it is clear that it was a sober and responsible contribution to the budget considerations. The idea of using taxation as a controlling element vis-à-vis pay increases was to be taken up in a wholehearted way over a year later, by the same Chancellor. This presents, of course, a different picture from that which was painted of the Research Department by others at later stages in the life of the 1974–79 administration. The tone of their advice was wholly one of caution, and an emphasis was placed on sorting out medium-term policy priorities, as well as on the need for fulfilment of certain important election pledges, like the increase in pensions.

This kind of medium-term perspective was lacking in Denis Healey's budget speech of 26 March. No time period for dealing with the massive balance of payments deficit was set. Emphasis was instead placed on the short-term defences that had been prepared for sterling. Borrowing amounted to some $5½–6½ billion; but half of this was on a short-term 'swap' basis, arranged with the Federal Reserve Bank of New York. The Chancellor was at pains to point out that the loans were not an easy way out: 'Borrowing is more sensible, in economic and human terms, than trying to cut imports by massive deflation, but no one should imagine that it is a soft option. The interest has to be paid each year, and this will eat into our surplus on invisible account.'[16] Import controls were mentioned too in the budget speech:

I have, of course, considered what direct measures I might take to narrow the balance of payments gap. I do not want to use direct restrictions on imports if this can be avoided; they would not be in the interests of the world economy, upon which we depend so much, and would invite retaliation. Moreover, they would have to be accompanied by measures to reduce home demand.[17]

Although it was no doubt prudent for any Chancellor in the position in which Mr Healey found himself at the beginning of 1974 to be a little vague about objectives like a target year for returning to a more normal balance of payments position, it should be emphasized that at that time no targeting of that sort had been done in the Treasury. So the Chancellor could not have given figures for a path of eliminating the non-oil deficit, had he wanted to. The three weeks which he had to prepare his budget gave enough time to establish the approximate size of the problems for 1974, and to put together a package that would achieve a certain number of well defined objectives. As things turned out, the idea given the Chancellor of the actual size of the public sector Borrowing Requirement for 1974–75 was so wrong (through sharply changing circumstances rather than poor forecasting) that it could well be argued that in some respects he had inadequate prior information for forming a budget judgement. Nevertheless, he took the opportunity of setting out with great clarity the principles which he intended should govern his future policy-making. He had inherited inflation of 13.2% (the year ending mid-February), and he had to make the alleviation of inflation one of the four touchstones of policy which he set out. But the principle which came first was the maintenance of full employment:

> I have been guided by four crucially important principles. First, we must make the fullest possible use of the manpower and resources available to us. I totally reject the philosophy that would cure high blood pressure in the economy by bleeding it to death. This principle means more than simply a high level of employment; it means a resolute attack on waste in every area of the economy – and our society too. We must not waste manpower or resources by leaving unused what we should use, or by treating scarce and expensive resources as if they were cheap and abundant. [18]

Besides dealing with inflation, the other two principles for policy were the achievement of a sustained improvement of the balance of payments, and re-creation of social unity through a fair division of the likely economic sacrifices and rewards the years to come would bring.

The budget kept faith with the responsible noises and pledges that had been made by the major industrial countries in the context of the oil crisis. It was the failure of the other countries similarly to pledge themselves against ardent deflation that was to provide one of the two major forces undermining the government's hopes over the following two years. The other force related to the hopelessly erroneous view initially taken of the public sector Borrowing Requirement, which measures the extent to which government spending exceeds current income. In turn, this had a great deal to

104

do with the laxity with which the government dealt with public sector pay claims in 1974 – since public sector pay made up such a large proportion of public spending it was, *ex post facto,* not surprising that massive pay settlements would upset the budget arithmetic.

Naturally, since the Labour politicians had made so much of their ability to get Britain back to work (the election slogan was 'Back to Work with Labour'), there was perhaps a good explanation for the increases in pay in some sectors – the mineworkers in particular. But massive pay settlements affected far more groups of employees than could have been justified in terms of ending the three-day week. It is worth considering the scale of these settlements before discussing the development of thinking in the period up to the spring budget of 1975.

From April 1974 to April 1975, the retail price index increased by 21.7%.[19] The New Earnings Survey of the Department of Employment[20] showed that in the year ending April 1975, average weekly earnings for all fulltime manual workers in all industries and services increased by 29.2% (weekly earnings including overtime). For manufacturing industries, the increase was less, 25.7%. However, on the same basis, weekly earnings in the public sector were substantially higher than this in a number of cases. Public administration manual workers got 33.2%, Local Authority administrative staff obtained 28.3%, teachers in Further Education obtained 43.2%, and teachers in primary and secondary schools received 39.8%. In the same survey, it was revealed that the miners had gained a 48.6% increase, including overtime, in average weekly earnings. The building industry provides the best contrast between wages attainments in the public and private sectors. Whereas in the private sector, construction workers obtained a 20.2% increase, including overtime, Local Authority building and civil engineering workers obtained a 32.6% increase.

There was good evidence to support the view that the bandwagon effect that had been expected to follow the miners' settlement was only really experienced in the public sector. Thus, the problems caused were substantially the result of decisions within the responsibility of the government itself.

Although the British budgetary measures had been cautious, it remained logical to call upon the other western nations to take positive action to avert the 'downside' risk. The increase in oil price could be viewed as entirely analogous to an imposition of an extra tax on oil in each major oil-consuming country. The OPEC oil surplus was equivalent in effect to a tax increase of some $65 billion or more, applied to all the OECD countries. As the McCracken Committee, set up at the OECD, reported in 1977:

This (oil) price increase generated increased export receipts to the oil-exporting countries from the OECD nations of around $65 billion per year. This increased import bill represented over 1½% of OECD GNP at that time, and considerably more for some individual countries (3 per cent for the United Kingdom, for example, and 3½ per cent for Japan).[21]

Thus the UK's national output had itself experienced a disproportionately large blow to growth, and the whole OECD area stood to lose up to 2% of output, if nothing were done to offset the effect. The dangers of attempts by the industrial countries to deflate and dump their oil deficits on others were well understood and explained by economists in the British Treasury, in the National Institute, and at the OECD in Paris. The OECD 'Economic Outlook' of July 1974 commented optimistically:

Initial fears of a scramble for current-balance positions have so far proved unfounded. At the recent OECD Ministerial meeting, all Governments conscious of the danger of conflicting attempts to improve national competitive positions, agreed upon a declaration stating their determination to avoid recourse, for a period of a year, to new restrictions on trade or other current transactions.

The Secretariat at the OECD at this time believed that the main problem would be one of recycling the massive sum of 'petro-dollars'. In a speech given on 9 September, the British Chancellor continued to emphasize the dangers of other countries not heeding the need to reflate:

If in addition to beggar-my-neighbour policies in world trade, Governments were to seek to reduce this rise in prices at home through massive reductions in demand beyond the reductions already imposed by the increases in oil prices, the current decline in economic activity could lead within two years to a world slump on the scale of the thirties. Although the signs of this danger are already mounting, I do not believe we will be so foolish. Indeed I was greatly encouraged in meeting some of my European and American colleagues in France this weekend by the universal recognition that it would be fatal to seek an answer to the problem of world inflation by creating a world slump. Mass unemployment is not regarded by any Government as an answer to our current problems. We must therefore take account of the deflationary impact of the petro-dollar surplus and accept the inevitability of massive payments deficits on oil account for some years to come.[22]

The Chancellor had taken various steps after his first budget to keep faith with the responsible sentiments of this speech. A clutch of measures had been announced in July, to bolster business confidence, and to offset the rising trend in unemployment. By doubling the Regional Employment Premiums, and adding further to food subsidies, it was hoped that the 'Social Contract' between the government and the unions would be reinforced. In November, yet a further 'mini-budget' was delivered, this time concentrating on helping the company sector with the much discussed liquidity crisis. The policy of 'borrowing through' the oil deficit problem was continued – and in July the Chancellor had been able to announce a further addition to his stock of loans, from an unexpected source: $1,200 million had been made available as a line of credit from the Shah of Iran. A very large portion of the OPEC funds had in any case found their way to London in 1974, thus making the problems of the British deficit deceptively easy to fund. The OECD 'Economic Outlook' estimated in December 1974 that liquid funds amounting to $14½ billion had been placed in London by the OPEC countries in the first nine months of the year. There was a sharp reversal of this favourable development at the end of the year, however. The massive favourable inflows of capital diminished, and there was a net private capital outflow, which forced the government to dip into its foreign credit.

Although the second 1974 election campaign tended to focus attention away from the gathering international crisis, the Chancellor was still keen to draw attention to his own efforts in persuading the other countries to counter the encroaching recession. But he was well aware that Britain was in a relatively weak position to persuade others. As he pointed out during the election campaign:

I'm afraid that unemployment is likely to rise during the

winter, and could rise through next year unless I do something about it. There is a problem for a country which has the inheritance which I incurred leading the world in reflation. And this is why I spent so much time in the last six months, trying to persuade some of my colleagues abroad that the cut in world demand of ninety billion dollars – eighty billion dollars this year, produced by the petro-dollar surplus, should not be multiplied and aggravated by domestic policies of deflation.[23]

The Chancellor went on to explain that there were plenty of signs that other countries were being responsible by taking expansionary measures. However, in his speech at the Labour Party Conference in November, he noted that other countries seemed to be slipping into recession faster than Britain:

I gave £200 million in my July measures and doubled the regional employment premium; and that I am certain is one reason why the rate of unemployment has been falling in Britain when it has been rising everywhere else in the world. Look at France and Germany – the last month we have figures for is September. There, their unemployment rose ten times more than ours did in Britain. And that is something you should be grateful to your Labour Government for.[24]

It was only at the very end of 1974 that it became clear that the other major OECD countries were not following the various exhortations to offset the recession. The most important – the United States and Germany – were plunging rapidly into extremely deep recession. The extent that this left Britain conspicuously exposed is illustrated in the following tables, derived from statistics prepared and published by the OECD Secretariat.

In mid-1974, following the various avowals of good faith and international solidarity, the picture of world growth, and the consequent share of the oil deficits was as shown in table 13.

So even with a sharp recession, Britain was expected to pick up one quarter of the total OECD deficit in 1974. In fact the various government measures did prevent Britain's downturn being a sharp 2% contraction. Other countries made the opposite adjustment. Instead of falling back by ½%, the US economy fell back 2%. Instead of moving forwards by about 2%, the German economy only achieved 1½%, as it plunged into sharper recession still in 1975. Table 14 shows the final outcome.

Table 13:    *International economy – forecast for 1974*[25]

| | Forecast 1974, Current Account Balance of Payments billions of dollars | Forecast GNP Growth %, 1974 on 1973 |
|---|---|---|
| US | −1.0 | −½ |
| Japan | −7.75 | −1½ |
| France | −6.2 | 4¾ |
| W. Germany | 7.0 | 1¾ |
| Italy | −8.75 | 3½ |
| UK | −9.75 | −2 |
| OECD TOTAL | −38½ | 1 |

Table 14:    *International economy – outcome for 1974*

| | Outcome 1974, Current Account Balance of Payments billions of dollars | GNP Growth % 1974 on 1973 |
|---|---|---|
| US | −0.87 | −2.1 |
| Japan | −4.69 | −1.8 |
| France | −5.9 | 3.9 |
| W. Germany | 9.34 | 0.4 |
| Italy | −7.92 | 3.4 |
| UK | −9.0 | −0.2 |
| OECD TOTAL | −34 | −0.1 |

So in total, the OECD area had come to a halt, with some nations managing to reduce their deficits much faster than anticipated – or in the case of Germany, actually managing to increase the anticipated balance of payments surplus. Only France and Italy among the major countries ended up with any appreciable growth in the year – with the consequence that, together with Britain, they accounted for two thirds of the area's overall payments deficit. Naturally enough, by 1975 they opted for policies that would quickly rid themselves of the massive burden, that had been expected to be fairly shared. Table 14 shows how quickly other countries in the OECD area plunged into recession at the end of 1974 – while the UK was still acting to keep the economy going. The net result of all this was that in 1975, Britain was clearly out of phase with all the other countries, and collected an enormous deficit at a time when the major countries moved either close to balance or to large surplus. Thus, in 1975 instead of a massive OECD area deficit of $15 billion, the area had a deficit only to the extent of $5½ billion. Britain, however, still had a deficit of nearly $4 billion, that was the natural result of being the slowest country to ditch the gentleman's agreements of the year before. Table 15 (opposite) shows how the scene was expected to develop, as at mid-1975, and how it actually did develop.

It was not surprising that, having rid themselves of their 'oil deficits' by deflating in a way they had solemnly said they would not, the major world economic powers seemed not to care very much about Britain's problem. Indeed, Britain was being regarded as less deserving of help, especially since pay settlements in early 1975 were seen to be out of control, and Britain did not appear to conservative-minded bankers to be doing enough to stop living 'beyond its means'. The highly publicized public sector Borrowing Requirements were also seen to be proof of rampant profligacy.

Having not planned a campaign for dealing with the balance of payments situation in such circumstances, the Treasury was therefore ripe to be taken wherever the whims of international finance should wish to take it – since the traditional hatchet of sterling balances still hung over all policy decisions. 'Sterling balances' represent capital lodged in London which can be withdrawn at any moment. If anything, the dangers of having policy suddenly changed as a result of short-term capital flows were greater as a result of the 'favourable' capital flows to London in 1974. The 'cushion' of

Table 15: *International economy – comparison of forecast and outcome for 1975*[26]

| | 1975 (Forecast) | | 1975 (Outcome) | |
| --- | --- | --- | --- | --- |
| | Current Account Balance, Billions of dollars | GNP % Growth, '75 on '74 | Current Account balance, Billions of dollars | GNP % Growth '75 on '74 |
| US | 3 | -3¾ | 11.7 | -2 |
| Japan | - ½ | 1½ | -0.7 | 2.2 |
| France* | -1¾ | 1 | 0.3 | -2.4 |
| W. Germany | 8 | -2 | 3.7 | -3.4 |
| Italy* | -1¾ | -2¾ | -0.6 | -3.7 |
| UK* | -3¾ | - ½ | -3.8 | -1.6 |
| OECD TOTAL | -15 | -1½ | -5.5 | -1.3 |

* GDP

international credit had paradoxically allowed the government to be taken deeper into a very old-fashioned trap.

As industry began to stagnate and unemployment mounted in the latter part of 1974, two obsessions gripped the senior personnel of the Treasury. One was to 'stop Benn'. The other was to prepare the ground for a tough incomes policy. The old favourite of senior officials had been brought out and renamed many times over the previous twenty years, as we have already noted. Sometimes a 'freeze', sometimes a 'pause', sometimes a 'guiding light' – the logic of pay policy had changed little. Nevertheless, it should be emphasized that a pay policy was entirely in tune with a Keynesian analysis of 'macro' policy options. Officials showed their hand formally on pay policy at the very end of 1974 when they recommended a tough pay policy to the Chancellor.

The fight over Labour's industrial policy had been hot from shortly after the arrival of the Labour government in power. Two factors worked in favour of the civil servants' intention to block proposals to carry out the spirit of Labour's programme in this area. First, many Labour ministers were opposed to an active industrial policy. Several ministers who were not particularly opposed to an industrial policy were extremely antipathetic towards Tony Benn, and thus were quite prepared to work with civil servants to undermine his proposals one way or another.

Secondly, the actual implementation of Labour's policies as in 'Labour's Programme' was less easy to formulate in a climate of crisis and panic than had perhaps been imagined by those who had drawn up the principles. Planning agreements had been seen as central to an industrial policy that would involve a systematic plan for industry as a whole. Various ministers, acting with the Whitehall machine, made sure that such planning agreements would not be compulsory. Nor would financial aid in general be related to participation in a planning agreement at the company level. Once it was established that there would be no real advantage for a firm from taking part in this central feature of the industrial policy, it is not surprising that virtually no firms did take part. The only planning agreement signed with a company outside the public sector was with Chrysler (UK), after the generous help given that concern by the government, following the ingenious Harold Lever's participation in negotiations. Having obtained millions from the British government, Chrysler later sold the UK operations to Peugeot of

France. The industrial policy was thus effectively sabotaged by Labour ministers in concert with like-minded civil servants. It nevertheless took time and care to carry out a U-turn of this magnitude. It was June 1975 before the Prime Minister felt it was safe to dance on the grave of industrial policy:

> Finally, in June, with the referendum over, Wilson was able to remove Benn from the D.I. [Department of Industry]. Victor Knight, political editor of the Sunday Mirror, who had predicted on 11 May 1975 that Benn would be moved after 5 June, remembers Wilson calling in some lobby correspondents for a special briefing. Wilson said he was going to put a stop to 'Bennery' once and for all.[27]

This certainly has the authentic flavour of the Whitehall attitude towards Tony Benn himself, and towards industry policy in general. With the Prime Minister leading from the rear, small wonder that the Chancellor should be a willing battering ram against those same objects of suspicion – even if he was himself potentially in favour of a micro-policy towards industry.

The TUC, which for years had been in principle favourable towards a more active government role in industry, was noticeably quiescent while Labour's industrial strategy was being diluted to nothing. This also highlights the fact that many leaders of the union movement were not actually serious in pursuing much more than token action from the government on the industrial front. They may have assumed that something real was being prepared – certainly Jack Jones reacted with great irritation a year later to the lack of policy on investment, and the general lack of industrial direction. However, by late 1975 the match was played and lost.

In the period up to the first election in 1974, the 'Social Contract' had been presented in various slightly different ways. The broad public impression was that the Labour Party had an agreement with the trade unions that they would exercise considerable restraint in pay bargaining, in return for certain key concessions and policies from a future Labour government. The main items to be expected from government were the end of various limitations and statutory powers exercised by government over pay negotiations, improved legislation on various aspects of employment, and a number of government actions to improve the 'social wage'. Among these, a most important item for one highly significant trade-union leader,

Jack Jones, was the higher state pension.

The incoming Labour government was able to fulfil many of its commitments – but the return for these actions was ill-defined when it came to the crunch. It was June before TUC General Council adopted a document that made its policy of self-restraint more clear. The key section of this was as follows:

> In summary, the General Council's recommendations to negotiators in the coming period are as follows:
> (i)   although the groundwork is being laid for increasing consumption and living standards in the future, the scope for real increases in consumption at present is limited, and a central negotiating objective in the coming period will there-fore be to ensure that real incomes are maintained;
> (ii)   this will entail claiming compensation for the rise in the cost of living since the last settlement; taking into account that threshold agreements will already have given some compensation for current price increases. [28]

In June, the most up to date figures published for earnings related to April. These figures had indicated that earnings year on year, were going forward at about 14%. Considering that over the same period inflation had increased prices by about 15%, this was not so outrageous. There was no exaggerated concern in government in 1974 about the way wages were moving. The very ferocity of the Conservative campaign in October over a pay and prices explosion encouraged ministers to find reasons for projecting confidence over how well the Social Contract was working. It was only in September, in any case, that figures revealed wage rates to be going up at over 20% – and even then, that evidence was not exactly conclusive, as independent commentators pointed out. Dominic Harrod, of the BBC explained:

> The big jump in basic weekly rates of pay comes from the national agreement reached earlier in the year by the engineering unions and from more threshold payments of up to 40p a week paid to some workers in August. A more reliable guide to what's actually happening, because it takes into account overtime, or the lack of it, is the average earnings figures also published today up to July. The rise in earnings was nearly 18 per cent compared with a rise in the cost of living of just over 17 per cent in the same twelve months. [29]

However, the prominence given to the Labour Chancellor's figures for inflation during the election campaign was unfortunate in that it portrayed a level of complacency that did not exist. The Conservative election manifesto had stated: 'Over recent months prices have been rising at an annual rate of over 20 per cent, and on present policies they will rise as much next year. This means that in two years the pound will be worth only 55p.' It is an arithmetical necessity that for prices to reduce the value of a currency by 45% in two years, an annual rate of inflation of over 25% is required. Nothing like that had occurred in the first six months of Labour government – and monthly price rises before the second election had been small.

This had partly been the result of budget action taken by the Chancellor, Denis Healey. He made great play of the exaggerated picture of inflation in 'recent months' that had been given by the Conservatives. Speaking at a Labour Party press conference on 23 September, he pointed out the fact that the very recent price trends had been, if anything, favourable:

In the last three months Mr Heath was in power they were rising at an annual rate of 19 per cent a year. Over the whole six months we were in power to the end of August, they were rising at an annual rate of 16½ per cent a year; but they have been falling steadily since April and very sharply indeed since June as you will see from this chart, and in the last three months, June to August, they were rising at the rate of only 8.4 per cent a year. Now during this period the United Kingdom has been doing very much better getting the rate of inflation down than most of her competitors in the world. The latest figures published by OECD are those from May to July so they do not include the dramatic reduction we had in August, and they show that whilst our rate of inflation was falling the rate of inflation was rising in the United States, in Canada, in France, in Italy, in Belgium, in Denmark, in Sweden, in Switzerland, and in Australia. Ours was falling when theirs was rising; and although our rate of inflation is still far too high, the rate of inflation in those months was higher still than ours in France, in Italy, in Belgium, in Denmark...

Now there are no grounds for complacency in the record which I have outlined to you from international statistics. The increase in world prices will continue to feed through into the shopping basket in Britain at least until the end of this year and the effect of threshold agreements will be raising prices up to about Easter next year and I'd be the last to deny that we in Britain still have some very formidable problems ahead. [30]

Britain's record on pay and prices for the whole of 1974 was not at all bad compared with other industrial nations, as figures published by the OECD showed:

Table 16: *Percentage increases in consumer prices and hourly earnings (manufacturing), 1973–1974* [31]

|  | Consumer Prices | Hourly Earnings |
|---|---|---|
| Canada | 10.9 | 13.4 |
| US | 11.0 | 8.4 |
| Japan | 24.5 | 26.3 (monthly) |
| France | 13.7 | 18.6 (rates) |
| W. Germany | 7.0 | 10.6 |
| Italy | 19.1 | 22.4 (rates) |
| UK | 16.0 | 17.0 |
| Belgium | 12.7 | 21.2 |
| Netherlands | 9.6 | 18.0 (rates inc. construction) |
| Denmark | 15.3 | 22.9 |
| Ireland | 17.0 | 20.3 |

It was early 1975 before a major change in emphasis was evident in government pronouncements on pay and inflation. The Chancellor had been warned at the very end of 1974 that prospects for inflation in 1975 were very bleak; as Joe Haines has pointed out, Treasury officials were so concerned with developments that: 'by the New Year of 1975 they were suggesting to the Chancellor of the Exchequer that the Government should put a terminal date on the current phase of the Social Contract – under which some trade unions were justifying the most extravagant pay claims'. [32]

At the beginning of 1975, the Chancellor of the Exchequer was still blaming the rising level of unemployment on the world situation:

> The main cause of our unemployment is the world recession and that is unlikely to get better this year. If we in Britain are to get through to 1976 without the sort of unemployment which already exists in the United States and Germany, three things are necessary:
>
> First we must have a lower level of wage settlements. This means sticking more strictly to the guidelines laid down by the TUC as part of the Social Contract.[33]

He was clearly beginning to hint that adherence to pay limitation should be a precondition for stopping unemployment rising.

David Basnett, General Secretary of the General and Municipal Workers Union was always regarded as a key figure by ministers in their relations with the trade-union movement. If it was going to be necessary to gain union support for a change in policy on wages, Basnett's opinion was a highly significant element in calculations. In early 1975, he apparently believed that the Social Contract was working:

> And I think, again, there is evidence that as far as its wage guidelines are concerned it's worked. We haven't seen the type of wage explosion after the statutory incomes period that we saw for instance in 1969. We haven't had any major industrial confrontation and, according to the Chancellor, the majority of settlements are within the guidelines. One of the values of the Social Contract, is its consensus means of trying to solve our problems.[34]

Up to spring 1975, the Labour government had been blaming world prices for the acceleration in prices in Britain – and as has been shown above, many other countries were suffering from high levels of inflation in 1974. Unemployment was also blamed on the level of world recession. But from the time of the spring budget of 1975, some of these relationships were inverted. Instead of being praised for being 'broadly within' the pay guidelines, the unions were blamed for the level of inflation that existed. And the rising level of unemployment, instead of being blamed on the world recession, was blamed on the level of inflation caused by the transgressions of the Social Contract. The Chancellor justified this explanatory U-turn in his budget speech:

117

The major source of this inflation for most of last year was the increase in world prices to which oil made such a contribution. But for many months now the prices of most metals and nearly all industrial materials have tended to fall. The price of most imported foodstuffs has, except sugar and beef, been fairly stable. The price of crude oil to the United Kingdom has been much the same since mid-1974. So for the last six months or so the main cause of rising prices in Britain has been the scale of wage and salary increases.[35]

Nevertheless, as the Chancellor stated, the effect of his spring budget was to *increase* prices: 'Mainly by adjusting the excise duties to reflect past inflation, my Budget measures themselves will put up the RPI [retail price index] by 2¾ per cent. This means that for some months yet we must expect high figures for the RPI compared with twelve months previously.' In his concluding remarks, he emphasized the fact that it had been a failure to contain inflation that had led to the unpalatable deflationary budget: 'But in this situation the key to our immediate success is the rate of inflation inside Britain, and it is our failure here which is responsible for the special severity of this Budget.'

Speaking about the budget, Denis Healey noted that settlements above the Social Contract level had been creating unemployment.

And the result is that I was prevented, I am afraid, from doing this [stimulating the economy] by the failure of too many working people, by no means all of them, I doubt whether more than 40 per cent of the settlements have been above the Social Contract, but of course, those that have, have been way above and this really has been throwing people out of work. Then an excessive wage settlement in one area means throwing people out of work in another.[36]

We can detect a subtle shift of thinking towards pre-war Treasury homilies.

As has been noted already, some of the most excessive wage settlements had in fact been agreed by ministers for workers in the public sector. Nevertheless, accusations tended to suit the occasion.

The deflationary spring budget was also argued for on the grounds that Britain was not paying her way in the world. The phase of

118

'recycling petrodollars' was necessarily given up and forgotten, since the other major countries had opted to deflate their balance of payments problems away. Britain was left holding the 'baby' – a massive deficit on payments, the inevitable consequence of keeping some life in the economy while others were plunging into deep recession.

Meanwhile, pay and prices were showing every sign of accelerating into high double figures. Nevertheless a mood of complacency was evident in May, in some quarters of government, as the following shows:

> PETER JAY: The pound is slumping to new lows, inflation rises month by month, unemployment is rising by 30,000 a month and predicted to reach a million before very long. Output is stagnating and we're borrowing something like 5p in every pound that we're spending from abroad, and the Cabinet, people say, seems to be at sixes and sevens...In short, we appear to be going on the rocks. Who, Mr Wilson, is at the helm?
>
> HAROLD WILSON: I am, but I've been away for two weeks at what has been the most successful Commonwealth Conference, 33 nations, that I have ever attended. While I've been away in fact nothing has happened, there hasn't been a single new index published, but I come back and I find not only journalists, commentators, but some politicians rushing round like wet hens as though some devastating crisis has hit the country.[37]

The sterling crisis which developed in mid-1975 finally forced a stronger government line on pay and prices. The policy which emerged was a joint policy with the TUC.

It was clear that the trade-union leaders understood the seriousness of the sterling crisis and were agreeing that pay was connected with the government's problems. They were persuaded that by a sacrifice on pay other aspects of policy would be saved. Jack Jones was the chief architect of the new agreement. However, his understanding of the crisis was coloured by the explanations given him by Treasury ministers, as the following quotation illustrates:

> JACK JONES: You see, take this question of unemployment. There is a great question of borrowing from abroad in large terms and this government's confidence has got to be sufficient

119

to attract the necessary borrowings to maintain our essential public services. Now it doesn't do that. And this is why the time factor is so very important from Denis Healey's angle. If the government doesn't do that it cuts public services, and that means unemployment, and unemployment, further massive unemployment, will reduce our negotiating abilities. And that in effect will be far worse than a wages policy.

INTERVIEWER: So you see your own plan as being a very essential part of the recapturing of foreign confidence?

JACK JONES: Yes. Most certainly. We've got to recapture foreign confidence, if we're going to maintain our levels of public spending on the essentials ... We've been boasting about the increase in the social wage in Britain, and do very well in that respect compared to many other countries. [38]

Jack Jones's £6 flat rate policy which was accepted later at the TUC in September, did in fact rescue the Labour government from the mid-year sterling crisis. After saving the government over pay, Jack Jones strongly supported proposals for an investment fund, put together by John Hughes, Director of the Trade Union Research Unit, at Ruskin College, Oxford. A meeting between a Treasury team led by Lawrence Airey, and a trade-union group took place in July. The trade-union team found the Treasury 'disturbingly negative and destructive' in their response to the proposal. [39]

Despite this kind of rebuff, the trade-union movement in general continued to give the government the benefit of its confidence and support. The main document supporting the Jack Jones proposal at the TUC placed great emphasis on the progress of the Labour government: 'The General Council have registered their dissent from some aspects of the April Budget, particularly those which will affect prices and unemployment [i.e. increase them]...Even so, the Movement should acknowledge the many steps taken by the Government in accordance with their undertakings.' Much was made of the Trade Union and Labour Relations Act, and the rise in the 'social wage.' Legislation on a wealth tax was 'expected in the 1976 Budget.' [40]

In the same document emphasis was once more placed on planning agreements and import controls: 'There is also a case for introducing more widespread import controls on manufactured goods as a temporary measure until the economy begins to expand again...Imports should be covered in planning agreements.' It is clear in retrospect that once the General Council had nailed its colours to pay restraint, it was going to be in a very weak bargaining position. Jack Jones himself, as the quotation above shows, was well aware how weak the trade-union position was likely to become if there was mass unemployment. The theme 'living beyond our means' is a traditional one for British Chancellors. Most often, it has been used to refer to the gap between imports and exports – the gap being measured by the 'current account' of the balance of payments. When imports have exceeded exports, it is logically simple to appeal to the common-sense notion that we are selling to the world less than we buy from it. The fact that sometimes the rest of the world may allow this or even wish it to happen is never alluded to by Chancellors. This latter possibility is fairly relevant to Britain in the early 1970s, since the importation of oil rigs was largely paid for by oil companies 'importing' the necessary finance. The oil companies of course knew that the importation of an oil rig was a necessary prelude to the production of oil – but the masochistic drive of British officials and media rarely allowed this elementary fact to be accepted.

An example of this current balance fetishism was provided by one senior Treasury official who, in the early phase of the 1974–79 government urged against policies to encourage high investment on the very grounds that these would increase imports, and thus increase the 'current account' deficit. Quite how substantial growth in productive capacity was going to be obtained without extra investment he never explained.

The other cause for which Chancellors rebuke the country for 'living beyond its means' relates to public expenditure. The gap between that which is raised in taxes, and that which is spent on government running costs and public projects is called the 'Public Sector Borrowing Requirement'. To the extent that the government funds this by issuing cash rather than interest bearing paper, the money supply is given an addition – but the change in money supply in any given year is never exactly equal to this addition. The depth to which the British economy plunged in 1975 necessarily increased the PSBR – since higher unemployment led to fewer people paying tax, and more people drawing the dole. Furthermore, the government's profligacy in pay awards in the public sector also substantially increased the debt to be financed. The scale of PSBR which the Chancellor announced in his spring budget had been unprecedented: £7600 million for 1974–75, and £9000 million in view for 1975–76.

Anxiety about the effect that this figure might have upon foreign holders of sterling was considerable – but Treasury advice had been that it was manageable from an internal point of view, if it was only temporary. It was politically embarrassing, particularly for Denis Healey as, in opposition, he had made much of Barber's deficits in accounts. We have noted that he had traded particularly upon the schism between the monetarist Conservatives behind Enoch Powell, and the more pragmatic Heath supporters.

For various reasons, therefore, he was anxious to sound a little monetarist 'at the edges' in late 1975. But as late as his speech to the Labour Party Conference in September 1975, he was pointing out that other countries had very high public sector deficits:

> This year, as a Government, as local authorities, as nationalised industries, we are spending ...10p in the pound more than we are getting in taxes, in rates, in fares, in charges for the nationalised industries. I believe we were right to do this, because if we had not we would be facing unemployment on the scale they have got in the United States. And the fact that we are right, I think, is proved by the fact that many governments which criticised us a year ago for the action which we took are now following our example.
>
> I got the figures out the other day. The deficit in United States local government and national government, as a percentage of national wealth, is nearly as high as ours. In Germany and Italy it is much higher. [41]

Despite these comments, he had been busy in the Treasury since mid-1975 preparing for a campaign to obtain massive public expenditure cuts from Cabinet. Cabinet members only learned of his preparations at the time of the Labour Party Conference when a senior official outside the Treasury informed his own Secretary of State of the Treasury's plans, to the Treasury's alarm.

The Chancellor ceased to point out the impact of counter-recessionary policies on the scale of PSBR after the conference. The focus of his attack on spending became the profligacy of local government:

> DENIS HEALEY: so that the amount of unplanned increase in expenditure which contributed to that 5 billion [of deficit] was about...20% of the total, and largely in the local authorities

which no government succeeded in controlling. In the last three to four years...the increase in their spending has been twice as much as the Government planned.

PETER OPPENHEIMER: Well, does that suggest that the new relations between local authorities and the Treasury or the Central Government will have to go beyond the consultative...

DENIS HEALEY: I think we shall have to apply cash limits to the rate support grant and we are discussing precisely how to do that now. And indeed in many areas of public expenditure, we've decided that control of programmes which have already been planned and agreed cannot be effective unless there's a limit in money terms. [42]

The 'limit in money terms' was to evolve into the 'cash limits' system, which did actually provide a closer control upon spending. It also had the virtue of sounding tough, and sounding like the embodiment of a monetarist principle.

The key change in stance in 1975 was towards unemployment. The 1975 budget was the first statement of Labour policy in two decades that had admitted that one of its consequences would be to increase unemployment. Healey said: 'The budget measures will reduce demand in 1975 by about £330 million and may be responsible for about 20,000 out of the total unemployed – about a fiftieth of the million. But this is part of the price we have to pay for inflation at current levels.'[43] Thus a fundamental commitment of both Conservative and Labour governments in the post-war era, dating from the 1944 White Paper, was dropped. The budget contained nothing to deal with the inflation which the Chancellor was anxious to portray as the root cause for his new course. In fact, the budget added to the inflationary problems: '...my budget measures themselves will put up the RPI by about 2¾ per cent.'[44] Unemployment at the end of 1975 was to be 428,000 worse than at the beginning of the year, standing at 1,371,000 in December.

Throughout 1975, as British unemployment rocketed skywards and output fell catastrophically, a long debate took place inside the Treasury over major strategic options. It has since become clear that the option most favoured by the more benign Keynesians at the Treasury – devaluation of the pound sterling – was that which eventually won the day. As might have been expected, the Bank of England was hostile to the devaluation strategy, but the events of 1976 showed that the Bank was temporarily overruled.

The policy of deliberate, but gradual devaluation started in the spring. By June 1976, it seemed that the devaluation strategy had got out of control. The President of the Netherlands Central Bank, Dr Jelle Zijlstra, contacted the Governor of the Bank of England to start organizing a reversal of the pound's fall.

Zijlstra's initiative marked the end of a bitter argument within the British Government over an economic strategy that was never publicly discussed. First, the fall in the pound, headlined week after week as disaster, had begun as deliberate official strategy; the trouble was that it had got out of hand. Second, there had been a fierce wrangle in Whitehall over whether it was either possible or desirable to stop the pound's fall, with just the kind of loan Zijlstra was proposing. The Treasury, which sponsored devaluation had maintained that nobody would lend us the money without conditions, and it was no use asking for it unless the Government was willing to change its economic policies.

Gordon Richardson [the Governor of the Bank of England] himself had no hesitation in his response to Zijlstra. He had always been less than enthusiastic about devaluation. [45]

Those inside the UK who wanted to see tough deflation imposed on the economy rather than the 'soft option' of devaluation had very powerful support abroad, particularly in the US. Ed Yeo, at the time Under Secretary for monetary affairs at the US Treasury, apparently regarded Britain as a kind of first barrier to protect the free world from financial chaos. Paradoxically he and his bosses at the US Treasury believed it to be their duty to make sure Britain was ensnared into total dependence on the IMF, and thus into contracting the UK economy. Interviewed on this issue he said: 'We feared that if a country like Britain blew up, defaulted on its loans, introduced foreign exchange controls and froze convertibility, we could have a real world recession.' [46] It remains rather puzzling what Mr Yeo thought had been happening in 1975 to the world economy.

Furthermore, the American views on government policy were simple, as Yeo indicated:

There is one fundamental fact about national economies. They have balance-sheets just like families or companies, and these have to show that income is not out of line with expenditure. The trouble in Britain was that people had a higher standard of living than the country was earning...

Our role was to persuade the British that the game was over. They had run out of string. [47]

It has been noted that Britain's determination to avoid triggering off the massive world recession had led the Chancellor to postpone deliberate recessionary policies in 1974. The US on the other hand, had played a big role in dragging the major economies down.

In any event, following the series of sterling crises later in 1976, the 'deflators' won the day. Once alternative policies, such as import controls as recommended by some in 1975, had been ruled out, it can be seen that the failure of 'Keynesian' devaluation of 1976 meant the end of positive policies for growth and reconstruction. With simple money men in charge of the purse strings, it was perhaps natural for British politicians to make a virtue out of crude monetarism, and gross over-simplifications in explanations to the populace became the order of the day.

It seems most logical to suppose that the public expenditure cuts announced early in 1976 were the mechanism by which the Treasury felt it was 'covering its flank' against the charge from conservative bankers that policy was dangerously profligate, or worse, in some way socialist. But the explanations given for the cuts at the beginning of the year were couched in terms that were perhaps too positive for the international taste. Space was being made for manufacturing expansion, it had been argued then, by holding government expenditure still: 'Faced with the need to keep income tax down and to strengthen our manufacturing industry the Government has decided that public spending should mark time once the coming year is over and unemployment is going down.'[48]

By the time of the mid-year crisis and shortly before the imposition of further expenditure cuts, imagery was used that the likes of Ed Yeo ought to have appreciated rather more:

Next year for example we expect to see manufacturing industry, and the basic industries seeking new funds to carry out fresh and enlarged programmes of new investment in plant and machinery. These industries are the wealth creators and they will be in competition with local and central Government for the available funds. Two buckets will be dipping into the pool

125

of savings. One is labelled 'Public Expenditure'. The other is labelled 'New Plant and Machinery'. Both will be scooping from the same pool, and Government will see that manufacturing industry gets a proper share of the pool without running into a new round of inflation.[49]

The Prime Minister, while being positive about manufacturing industry, appeared not to know that the 'pool' could vary in size, depending on what the government did. His statement contained the essence of pre-war 'static' economics.

But once the toughness of the Americans and others had been encountered in the guise of the IMF loan negotiations, there was talk of 'redeploying' people, not just savings. In the words of BBC's Angela Rippon:

And with negotiations with IMF now at a crucial stage, a Treasury Minister, Mr Joel Barnett, has warned that large numbers of people will have to leave their jobs in central and local government to work in industry. In the last ten years, Civil Servants and local government workers have increased by more than a quarter of a million, while industry has lost a million workers. Mr Barnett says public spending has grown faster than the rate of economic growth can sustain, and this has been a major reason for Britain's economic decline.[50]

The sterling crisis had helped the Labour government in pay negotiations with the trade unions, and with weak sterling and a recovering world economy in 1977, prospects should have been moderately good. Unfortunately, the cuts and panic of 1976 had in the short run cut growth rate prospects. More seriously, they had broken the nerve of policy-makers, and placed them under the constraint of the IMF, which was to dole out credit under rigid terms. Initiative had therefore been lost, in all major economic matters, for the next couple of years of Labour's tenure of office. Naturally, some rejoiced at this. *The Economist* of December carried a hideous cartoon of Denis Healey as a marionette, with the headline 'Strings Attached':

The good news on Wednesday was that the loan from the International Monetary Fund will be doled out in instalments up to some time in 1978, with audits to check whether Britain is fulfilling the loan's terms. This period of rule by IMF

126

Inspectorate-General should give the country better government than successive teams of British politicians have done; and it starts at an auspicious moment when sterling exchange rate is low and should be rising, while interest rates are high and should be falling. That should provide favourable conditions for controlling the money supply and balance of payments.

*The Economist* was not worried about unemployment running in the region of one and a half millions. It had already offered the comforting thought in May 1976 that unemployment would dampen wage demands and might 'free more Britons to become guest workers in Europe'.[51]

At the beginning of 1976 Healey had used references to monetarism in his budget speech to remind the Conservatives of their own divisions, without totally committing himself to the concept:

> Second, it remains my aim that the growth of the money supply should not be allowed to fuel inflation as it did under my predecessor. To this end, I aim to see that the growth of the money supply is consistent with my plans for the growth of demand expressed in current prices. If it became clear that this aim were not being achieved, I would be ready to use the appropriate mix of policies – not necessarily monetary policy alone – to redress the situation.[52]

As late as June that year, the Chancellor felt he could be quite dismissive of monetarism – as was shown in a television interview:

> ROBIN DAY: May I ask you whether you think that an addition to your armoury of weapons in restoring confidence, in addition to the pay deal, would be to fix, as many people advocate, a fixed level of the money supply which won't be exceeded?
> DENIS HEALEY: I don't think that would help – I've looked into this very carefully in countries which have one...Now I do ask you, Robin, monetarism is a very trendy drug at the moment, and some people have gone overboard for it, but it's not got very much more sense you know than many other drugs...But to fix a target, and to make that govern the rest of your policy, I don't think that makes sense.[53]

The Chancellor announced monetary targets in July 1976, and monetary control was made firmly part of the agreement later in the year with the IMF. Healey had opted for monetarism as the Treasury had given him no alternative. Its own option, gradual devaluation, had been pursued ineffectively and eventually had become a rout, thus discrediting the remaining Keynesians in positions of influence. The quotation at the beginning of this chapter certainly indicates the 'trial and error' nature of policy from 1974 to 1976, but as we shall see, there was no learning process involved.

## REFERENCES

1   Denis Healey, *Guardian*, 15 February 1979
2   *The Economist*, 29 October 1973
3   CSO Database
4   ibid.
5   OECD Economic Outlook, December 1973
6   NIESR Review, February 1974
7   Anthony Barber, speaking at Overseas Bankers' Club, 4 February 1974; *Financial Times*, 5 February 1974
8   IMF Communiqué; *New York Times*, 19 January 1974
9   NIESR Review, op. cit.
10  Denis Healey, Labour Party Press Release, February 1974 (GE38/74)
11  ibid.
12  Denis Healey, Labour Party Press Conference, February 1974
13  ibid.
14  Labour Party Research Department, 11 March 1974
15  ibid.
16  *Hansard*, col. 286, Budget Statement, 26 March 1974
17  *Hansard*, cols. 290–91, Budget Statement, 26 March 1974
18  ibid.
19  Monthly Digest of Statistics, CSO
20  The New Earnings Survey, April 1975; published in the *Department of Employment Gazette*, November 1975
21  'Towards Full Employment and Price Stability', OECD, June 1977
22  Denis Healey speaking at luncheon of the Conference Board, Hilton Hotel; Treasury Press Release, 10 September 1974

23   Denis Healey, speaking on Thames TV's 'People and Politics', 26 September 1974
24   Report of the 73rd Annual Conference of the Labour Party, 29 November 1974
25   OECD Economic Outlook, July 1975 (Tables 13 and 14)
26   ibid.
27   Tom Forester, *New Society,* 6 July 1978
28   TUC 'Collective Bargaining and the Social Contract'; adopted by TUC General Council, 26 June 1974
29   BBC Radio News, 18 September 1974
30   Labour Party Press Conference, 23 September 1974
31   OECD Economic Outlook, July 1975
32   Haines, Joe, *The Politics of Power*, Jonathan Cape 1977, p.44
33   Denis Healey, speaking at East Sussex Labour Party Rally; Labour Party Press Release, 22 February 1975
34   BBC Radio 4, 'Analysis', 27 February 1975
35   *Hansard*, col. 274, 15 April 1975
36   Labour Party Newstape No. 91, April 1975
37   LWT 'Weekend World', 11 May 1975
38   BBC 2 'Newsday', 26 June 1975
39   John Hughes, *Sunday Times,* 31 August 1975
40   The Development of the Social Contract, Supplementary Report A, TUC 1975
41   Labour Party Press Release, 30 September 1975
42   BBC Radio 4, 23 October 1975
43   *Hansard,* col. 320, 15 April 1975
44   *Hansard,* col. 318, 15 April 1975
45   Stephen Fay and Hugo Young, *Sunday Times* Weekly Review, 14 May 1978
46   ibid.
47   ibid.
48   Denis Healey, speaking at Failsworth; Labour Party Press Release, 27 February 1976
49   James Callaghan, speaking at the General and Municipal Workers' Conference, 7 June 1976
50   BBC 2 'Newsday', 26 November 1976
51   *The Economist*, 1 May 1976
52   *Hansard*, col. 237, 6 April 1976
53   BBC1 'Tonight Special', 11 June 1976

# 8

# Back to the 1920s

*Hegel remarks somewhere that all facts and personages of great importance in world history occur, as it were, twice. He forgot to add: the first time as tragedy, the second as farce.*
*Karl Marx*, The Eighteenth Brumaire of Louis Bonaparte, *1852*[1]

Before examining the development of the monetarist fashion from 1977 through to 1980, it is well worth reviewing in broad terms what happened to the British economy under the 'improved' IMF management welcomed so heartily by *The Economist* and others. The table on page 98 shows how quickly the UK economy recovered from the recession of 1970–71, to reach a high point of manufacturing output in 1973 that was not to be exceeded in any of the seven following years. Unemployment was at its lowest one year after the peak of the 'Barber boom', in 1974. Concern over the soaring unemployment rate was one of the motives for the initiative in 1976, when the competitiveness of British industry was restored to the level of 1973, and even improved compared with that year. It will be remembered that 1973 was the year in which the Conservatives' flotation of sterling had its largest impact on the relative price advantage of British manufacturers compared with overseas competitors.

The 1976 devaluation was, as we have noted, unaccompanied by any important measures to expand the economy, and within a matter of months, the IMF conditions placed the Chancellor in an uncomfortable monetary straitjacket. The public expenditure cuts, which had caused so much agony in Cabinet for so many months had no effect in transferring labour from the service sectors to manufacturing. Employment in manufacturing was 5% lower in 1978 than it had been in 1974. A small revival in manufacturing investment did take place, but even at the peak of this revival, in 1978, the investment in real terms was substantially less than that which had taken place in 1970, eight years before. The UK economy went into recession later than the other main economies (see Chapter 7) but under the monetary restraints of 1977 onwards, the British economy stayed down. Manufacturing output at the beginning of the election year of 1979 was lower than it had been at the end of 1976 when monetary control had been enforced. Only one industrial area was encouraging. This was North Sea oil, which proved to be a substantial handicap. This paradox related to the increasing sentiment that because of North Sea oil production, the City of London was a more secure place to funnel the world's supply of liquid capital. Despite the clear evidence of 1979 that Britain was spending the oil revenues as fast as they came in, anxiety about international oil supplies made foreign bankers only too willing to subsidize Britain's legendary proclivity to live beyond her means, by moving huge sums of money into sterling accounts in London.

So the only advantage to manufacturers left from the devaluation initiative of 1976 was eroded in 1977 and 1978, and had gone altogether by 1979. The squeeze that this imposed upon British manufacturers was intense. But the new Conservative Chancellor maintained that the stagnation of output and rising unemployment following his tougher version of monetarism were part of the treatment. Just as the Treasury knights of 1925 had argued that short-term hardship was essential for bringing down inflation and eventually restoring the economy to health, so the new Conservative administration argued that dealing with inflation was the highest economic goal, and that government could probably not affect unemployment anyway.

Denis Healey had prepared public opinion for this kind of simplistic view. While successfully negotiating a further phase of the voluntary pay policy, he had made it quite clear that he was not going to expand the economy, or take much account of TUC advice. He was, of course, in the IMF trap sprung after the 1976 disaster. In his New Year message for 1977, he had emphasized

131

that any growth that might come would have to be through exports, not through budgetary stimulus:

> I have set firm and severe targets for Domestic Credit Expansion and for the associated growth in monetary aggregates. This ensures that the prospect for exports will not, as sometimes in the past, be damaged by over-stimulation of domestic demand. But the new monetary targets will not in any way inhibit any growth which is generated by the balance of payments. [2]

In January 1977, *The Times* lauded harsh monetary control of the economy, and castigated those who in the past had tried for economic growth. Their leader provoked a most lucid response from a former Conservative Chancellor, Reginald Maudling:

> I was fascinated by your reference... to my 'crude fiscal and monetary expansionism'. As this has become part of the common jargon of those who, like you, have been captivated by the latest trend in monetary economics, I thought I might ask for a little elucidation. My Budget of 1963 was designed to achieve economic expansion at a time of heavy unemployment and under use of capacity, about which unions and management alike were complaining... Between the 1963 Budget and the fall of the Conservative Government in 1964, the money supply, to which you attach so much importance, in relation to GNP hardly varied. Output increased by nearly 15 per cent and inflation was at the rate of 4 per cent. I do not recall that the economic pundits of the press then criticised the degree of reflation which I introduced...
>
> You say that 'The acid question remains whether the Government, any Government, can go on indefinitely resisting the political pressure to move in this direction (i.e. reflation), even though it may take years before the effects of endemic recession on pay determination and work practices eventually begin to bring unemployment down.' What could be clearer than that?
>
> In the old days the slogan was, 'treat them mean and keep them keen'. Keep unemployment up, stagnation going, investment down indefinitely until the workers have learnt their lesson... This, in blunt language, is what you really mean... It is a point of view held by many people. It is central to the whole theme of monetary economics. [3]

Table 17: *The Pay Squeeze. Real weekly net income for average wage earner, 1973–74 to 1978–79*[4]

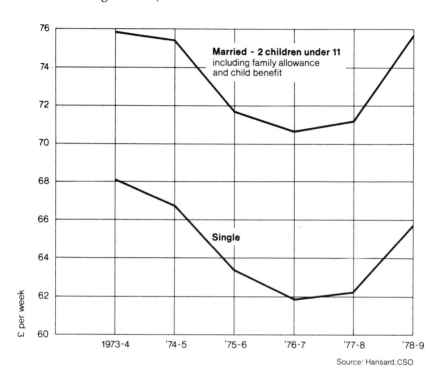

Source: Hansard, CSO

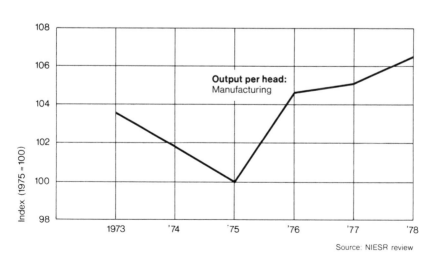

Source: NIESR review

Early in 1977 the Chancellor began to see advantages in reversing the sterling devaluation of 1976, despite the fact that this had been the linchpin of his expansionary hopes. In his budget speech in March, he looked forward to reversing his steps still further: 'The rise in the exchange rate from the low point it reached last October is worth about 3 per cent off the RPI by the end of this year. If, as I hope, my proposals today for income tax relief help get another round of pay policy accepted, that will help with the future level of the exchange rate and of prices.'[5]

The extent to which trade-union compliance had already been obtained is illustrated by the figures for real take home pay over this period of the Labour government's life, charted on page 000. These figures show that for a married man with two young children, the two successive rounds of pay policy reduced his purchasing power by 7% between the tax year 1974–75 and that of 1976–77. Inflation had actually fallen in 1976 from the rate it reached in 1975. The average increase in 1975 had been 24%, while in 1976 it fell to 16½%. In 1977, it fell again, although the Chancellor was still repining the damage done by his own devaluation strategy of 1976 at the Lord Mayor's Mansion House dinner in October 1978: 'Some people used to see depreciation as an easy way of restoring price competitiveness. But hard experience confirms the findings of economic research – that the price increases generated by a fall in the exchange rates are tending to feed through a good deal faster into rising labour costs than they used to. Depreciation can no longer be treated as a soft option.'[6]

At the same dinner, the Governor of the Bank of England made no bones about his own adherence to the 1920s dogma: 'Monetary policy is and must remain central to the restraint and ultimate defeat of inflation.'[7] The contribution to getting inflation down made by the trade unions seemed to have slipped the Governor's mind. The sacrifices made by many trade unionists in real income were ignored by the monetarists. Samuel Brittan, writing in the *Financial Times* on 25 January 1977 claimed that Jack Jones rated highly as an architect of unemployment, because of his instrumental role in the flat rate voluntary pay policies of 1975 and 1976. His argument was excellent vintage Treasury (1920s) form.

Manufacturing stagnation and the squeeze on real incomes of trade unionists were the seeds of destruction for the 1974–79 Labour government. The pay disputes of the winter of 1978–79 were the natural results of pent-up frustration. Trade unionists had not seen much in terms of a *quid pro quo* for their restraint up to then.

Once pay policy began to break down at the end of 1978, inflation began to pick up again. The average increase in the Retail Price Index in 1978 had been 8.3%. Despite appreciating sterling, and a continued tough monetary policy, inflation rose sharply in 1979, although this bitter pill was couched in terms of public expenditure cuts and massive direct tax reliefs. The new Conservative government eschewed pay policy, in line with the views of the monetary purists.

In his budget speech on 12 June 1979, Geoffrey Howe announced cuts in taxation, treating wealthier earners particularly favourably, as well as a programme of cuts in public expenditure. These measures were supposed to restore incentives and make room for industrial and commercial development: 'But those changes will not themselves be enough unless we also squeeze inflation out of the system. It is crucially important to re-establish sound money.'[8] Squeezing inflation out of the system was the great Treasury preoccupation in the 1920s, until it decided after the slump that falling prices were harmful. The return to gold, involving a substantial revaluation of sterling was another enthusiasm. Under Howe, the tight money policy led to massive inflows of short-term capital, pushing sterling up, and making many parts of British industry unprofitable and vulnerable to imports.

In March 1980 the Chancellor, Sir Geoffrey Howe, set out his simplistic economic philosophy concisely:

> Last year we made an important start on tackling that inheritance (the inheritance from Denis Healey). We set about reducing the rate of monetary growth. We achieved large reductions in dangerously oversized public spending plans. We reduced the share of Government spending and borrowing in the nation's output. And when, last November, the money target looked like being extended, we acted promptly and decisively. We have removed many unnecessary controls and obstacles to enterprise and individual effort.[9]

But what use could be made of individual effort in the middle of the major recession which Geoffrey Howe announced was imminent?

Professor Milton Friedman, the world's best known monetarist, became a kind of 'Godfather' to the new Conservative Cabinet, and came to visit Mrs Thatcher in London. But Friedman had been careful in the past not to claim too much for monetary policy. As he had written many years before: 'The first and most important lesson that history teaches about what monetary policy can do – and it is a lesson of the most profound importance – is that monetary policy can prevent money itself from being a major source of economic disturbance. This sounds like a negative proposition; avoid major mistakes. In part it is.'[10]

Monetarism and Friedman were fêted by the British media from 1977 to 1980. If the media did not understand economics, they certainly made up for it by their understanding of fashion. From the *Financial Times* to the *Guardian*, articles adopting monetarist standpoints flourished. Friedman and Samuel Brittan published pretentious open letters to one another in the *Financial Times*. Lengthy articles by Friedman appeared in the *Listener* and *The Times*. The theme that unemployment was the result of trade unionism, a favourite chestnut from the 1920s, appeared in many places including the *Guardian*'s 'Economic Notebook' in 1977. The trade unions were blamed for Britain's low economic growth by Samuel Brittan, a monetary convert, in the *Financial Times* in 1978. In 1979, an ex-Treasury official, Patrick Minford, published fulsome praise for the first Conservative budget, largely because: 'This is the first budget in this country drawn up explicitly according to monetarist principles. This budget heralds the start of a strategy which, if persisted in with determination and commitment, offers the promise of a return to a sound currency at a cost that we should be well willing to bear.'[11]

Sir Otto Niemeyer would have been proud of him.

A whole score of assorted gentlemen and academics signed an article published in *The Times* at the beginning of 1980, commencing with the assertion: 'Monetarism is the internationally recognised technique for trying [sic] to achieve what everyone wants – the end of inflation. It is not a nostrum of cranks. Only by mastering inflation can we hope to improve our economic performance and prospects for employment.'[12] Sir Otto Niemeyer would have been proud of them too.

In fairness to *The Times*, it should be pointed out that it also published an article later in the year which stated that the only place in the world to have attempted to apply Mr Friedman's principles for long had been Chile, and that there, monetarism and 'free market principles' had been introduced at the point of a gun, with wholesale repression, torture and arrests.[13]

However, not all commentators had been entranced by Professor Friedman. Writing about a long series of TV programmes dedicated to Professor Friedman and the 'Friedman' approach to economic policy, Chris Dunkley of the *Financial Times* said:

> Give me a film crew for several weeks, an editing suite for several more and a fairly hefty budget and I reckon I could make you half a dozen little filmlets which would suggest very convincingly that black was white and up was down...
>
> The programme demonstrated a decided imbalance of time in Professor Friedman's favour. Friedman had a fairly easy time in studio discussions with various invitees, chaired by convert to monetarism, Peter Jay.
>
> The only person I have seen who really rocked Friedman back in his chair was Charles Medawar who was invited by chairman Peter Jay, in his new Frostian mid-Atlantic drawl, to give an instance of the government protecting consumers in a way that market forces never would. Medawar did so, offering drugs as an example. Friedman trotted out a practised rejoinder from his 30-year American arsenal and Medawar promptly floored him by showing that the reply held good, if at all, only for American patent medicines and not for the British ethical drugs in the example. It was this kind of detailed analytical counter argument of which there has been far too little in the series, and for the first time the Professor looked disconcerted. For the rest of the time:

> ...he looked like a peddler
> just opening his pack,
> His eyes how they twinkled, his
> dimples how merry!

> ...A wink of his eye and a twist
> of his head
> Soon gave me to know I had
> nothing to dread'

which, for anyone who has watched the little man playing to the gallery week by week with his winks and his grins will seem a very accurate description though the words were actually used by another American, Clement Clarke Moore, to describe Friedman's spiritual twin – Father Christmas. [14]

REFERENCES

1   Marx, Karl, *The Eighteenth Brumaire of Louis Bonaparte*, 1852, reprinted Progress Publishers 1977 (7th printing), p. 10
2   *Financial Times*, 31 December 1976
3   Reginald Maudling, letter published in *The Times*, 20 January 1977
4   *Hansard*, 26 January 1979. Written reply by Robert Sheldon, Financial Secretary at the Treasury
5   *Hansard*, Budget Statement, March 1977
6   *Financial Times*, 20 October 1978
7   ibid.
8   *Hansard*, col. 241, 12 June 1979
9   *Hansard*, col. 1441, Budget Statement, 26 March 1980
10  Friedman, Milton, *The Optimum Quantity of Money and Other Essays*, Macmillan 1969, p. 106
11  *The Banker*, July 1979
12  *The Times*, 9 January 1980 – Messrs G. C. Allen, P. Bareau, S. Caine, W. Clarke, S. Dennison, B. Griffiths, R. Harris, G. Hutton, W. Letwin, P. Minford, V. Morgan, A. Peacock, I. Pearce, G. Pepper, H. Rose, A. Seldon, J. Wiseman, G. Wood, J. B. Wood, B. Yamey
13  *The Times*, 11 September 1980
14  Chris Dunkley, *Financial Times*, 19 March 1980

# 9

# Conclusion

*They have the wrong sort of good education – suitable for running an empire 80 years ago without nepotism or corruption; inadequate for running a great industrial nation today.*
*Edward Heath on civil servants, 1976*[1]

Senior civil servants tend to regard politics as a rather nasty business which goes on in the three weeks or so before a general election. The relevance of that rather unpleasant and undignified process for policy is held to be somewhat limited. Policy, on the other hand, is very much their business and, as has been noted elsewhere, they aspire to reach the policy-making layer as early as possible in their careers. Since many senior party politicians of today share the senior civil servants' views on these matters, it is not fair to accuse the civil servants of a 'conspiracy'. But we must note the grave disadvantages to policy of a system in which much of the real decision-making is being done by people drawn from a narrow social base, with negligible experience in important fields such as finance and industry, and facing almost no exposure to public criticism and debate. This final deficiency is most critical, since it is as true now as it was in Bagehot's day that the necessary bureaucratic processes for a democracy to work must allow refreshing criticism from outside. With the scale of our administrative machinery so much enlarged, it is clear that ministers do not have a chance of exercising that role.

Some have argued that the way to solve all these problems is to cut back on government activity and let market forces govern development in the economic field. The monetarists, so much in the height of fashion in the late 1970s, conveniently forget that the remedy has been tried before, and failed. That is not to say, however, that there is no such thing as market force; this has to be taken into account in policy. As Sir Alec Cairncross, at one time Chief Economic Adviser to the Treasury, wrote:

> Laissez-faire was a dogma rather than a fact: the State never yielded entirely to the general bias against intervention in industry. In particular, it showed more reluctance to leave domestic trade uncontrolled than to adopt free trade in international economic relations. The subsequent extension of government control, however, particularly over the last fifty years, represents something of a revolution in economic policy and it is no longer possible to treat such control as exceptional and running counter to the general temper of the age.²

Nevertheless, purely 'reactive' Keynesian policies have not prevented Britain's relative – and now absolute – decline. The policy options taken have frequently come to grief as a result of sterling's perpetually exposed position, and the City of London's role as an entrepot for 'hot money'. This yields benefits, but nothing equivalent to the cost of active recessionary policies frequently adopted by governments. Rarely have policy initiatives been pursued in a really dedicated manner. Officials ought to and no doubt do realize that the problem of dealing with sterling must precede active economic policies. The DEA and the National Plan, the Maudling 'dash for growth', the Barber boom, and the Healey devaluation were all initiatives which might have worked if the whole weight of the administrative machine had been committed to their success. They remain options which could be tried. But looked at from inside the 'ivory tower', why expose the reputation of the Treasury if there are going to be no great rewards for success? And moreover, why worry about gradual failure if it rebounds on the minister, not the institution?

In order to make sure that future initiatives succeed, there must be a change in the way that the machinery of government works; many possibilities exist. A move to a system of widespread political appointments to the Civil Service in the American style would be one. The institution of politically chosen 'Cabinets' in the French manner would be another. Perhaps senior civil servants could be allowed to register their political affiliations, so that a minister could place men and women in key positions who, *a priori*, could be expected to pursue his line with determination. Senior civil servants shift between jobs so often that an extra movement every four years or so would make little difference. It is in any case the fact that many senior civil servants today are willing, in confidence, to state their own political loyalties. Why should they not take their 'permanent' political role one step further, and let their own view be public?

[handwritten margin note: probably not]

Closer contact between civil servants and the real industrial and economic world is essential, yet greatly neglected. The City cannot be blamed for using its own advantageous geographical and traditional position to influence government. But officials certainly can be criticized for focusing their attention within the boundaries defined by the House of Commons, the 'Square Mile' and the Reform Club. This applies equally to ministers charged with handling Britain's economic policies.

Time will show that the route of monetarism leads nowhere, other than to higher unemployment and stagnation. While Professor Friedman tours the world explaining that it was misapplied monetarism at fault, not the doctrine, as he has said already about the depression in the US, over two million British workers will be out of work. The Treasury will be able to test another cherished hypothesis, and see if massive unemployment 'teaches organized labour a lesson'. It might be a rowdy tutorial – it is certainly an unnecessary one. A new and insensitive administration has given the unworldly mandarins an experimental opportunity which they have not had for fifty years. It is not possible to imagine a Thatcher or a Joseph showing the depth of perception of a Macmillan:

> I shall never forget those despairing faces, as the men tramped up and down the High Street in Stockton or gathered round the Five Lamps in Thornaby. Nor can any tribute be too great to the loyal, unflinching courage of the wives and mothers, who somehow continued, often on a bare pittance, to provide for husband and children and keep a decent home in being. Even in the South of England, the sight of wounded or unemployed ex-Servicemen begging in the street was now too common to be remarkable. Sometimes these demonstrations

of misery took a more organised but none the less distressing form, such as the 'hunger marches', as they came to be called. Of these, the march of the Jarrow unemployed was the most poignant; for with the closing of Palmer's shipyard, almost the sole means of employment in the town had come to an end. There was of course national, local, and individual relief and assistance, on a scale unequalled in the history of this or any other country. But charity, whether of the nation as a whole or from their neighbours, was not what the men wanted. They wanted work. The British economy was indeed sick, almost mortally sick, with a great part of its capital of machinery and manpower unused, and, in some areas, rotting away.[3]

The scale of Britain's industrial backwardness today is indeed intimidating. The nature of Britain's Civil Service élite has had an important part in relegating the problems of Britain's manufacturing base behind such issues as the short-term management of financial markets – their whole cultural bias makes this behaviour as inevitable in the 1980s as it was in the 1920s.

If a team such as that of the great French planner Monnet examined Britain's factories and industries today, it would no doubt come up with an inventory of backwardness similar to that which Monnet found in France in 1945. Monnet had said to de Gaulle at that time:

'I don't know exactly what has to be done: but I'm sure of one thing. The French economy can't be transformed unless the French people take part in its transformation. And when I say "the French people", I don't mean an abstract entity: I mean trade unionists, industrialists, and civil servants. Everyone must be associated in an investment and modernization plan.'

'That is what has to be done, and that is the name for it,' de Gaulle concluded. 'Send me your proposals before the end of the year.'[4]

It is quite impossible to imagine the Treasury administrators wishing to share major decisions in this way – their narrow experience and traditional arrogance has set them apart for at least the last fifty years. Their insularity from events abroad also makes their advice limited in range, and hardly commendable for its rate of success.

At the end of the day, our system dictates that the politicians must take the blame for policy failure, and that the civil servants are not accountable. Yet it is all too clear from the chapters above that our closed bureaucracy has harboured destructive doctrines for decades, and since the 1950s has tended to shield itself not only behind secrecy but behind recriminations over trade unions and the incompetence of politicians. It cannot be excused blame for the events which led the nation back to the crude monetary policies of the 1920s.

If future politicians are to succeed as brilliantly in overcoming the British economic malaise as did the French administrations after Monnet, then there is no shadow of a doubt that great changes must take place in the structure of economic decision-making. The present custodians have failed and, one way or another, must be replaced.

## REFERENCES

1  Edward Heath, *The Times,* 27 May 1976
2  Cairncross, Sir Alec, *Introduction to Economics*, 4th ed., Butterworths 1966, p. 550
3  Macmillan, Harold, *Winds of Change*, Macmillan 1966, p. 285
4  Monnet, Jean, *Memoirs* (trans. R. Mayne), Collins 1978, p. 234

# Index

147

Peugeot 112-13
Peyton, John 20
Pigou, A. C. 63
politicians 3, 11, 12
  accountability 7-8, 139
  civil servants and 3-4, 7-8
pottery industry 77
pound, fall of 6, 119
  floating of 89-90
  strength of 7, 33-4
  value of 49, 55, 115
  *see also* sterling
Powell, Enoch 122
prices 20, 36, 44-5, 54-5, 58-9,
  64-6 *passim,* 114-16 *passim,* 118, 119,
  127, 134
Private Consumption Expenditure 87,
  89
private enterprise 1
production 4, 53, 55, 58, 64, 65, 66, 72,
  74, 76, 97, 101, 130-32 *passim*
public expenditure 120, 121, 126, 135
  cuts in 6, 122, 125, 130, 135
Public Records Office 67, 79
public sector Borrowing Requirement
  103-4, 110, 121-2
Public Works Loans Board 77

Radcliffe Committee (1958) 34, 39
Rampton, Sir Jack 40-41
rates 123
rearmament 5, 11, 14-15, 42, 45, 50, 60,
  62-84
  German 69, 73
recession 55, 58, 65, 68, 99-100, 107,
  108, 110, 117, 119, 122, 124-5,
  130-32 *passim,* 135, 140
reflation 106, 108, 132
Regional Employment Premiums 107,
  108
Retail Price Index (RPI) 90, 105, 118,
  123, 134-5
revaluation 135
Ricardo, David 63
Richardson, Gordon 35, 124
Robinson, Austin 79
Roll, Sir Eric 20
Roosevelt, President Franklin D. 15
Roseveare, Henry 33-4
Rowe Dutton, Ernest 50
Royal Air Force 5, 68, 70-72 *passim*
  expenditure on 71-2, 74

Royal Commission on the Civil Service
  (1929) 14
Royal Navy 5
Russia 53
  Five-year Plan *(Gosplan)* 79-80

Sedgemore, Brian 19
service industries 2
Sharp, Baroness Evelyn 16-17, 19
Siepman, H. A. 33
Simon, Sir John 70
slump 106-7, 135
Smith, Adam 8, 63
Snowden, Philip 47
Social Contract 113-18
Standard Bank 37
state intervention 65, 76-7, 79, 81-2, 86,
  112, 140
steel 58, 68, 81, 101
sterling 4, 33, 45, 88, 94, 103, 110, 122,
  123, 130, 131, 134-5
  crises 7, 47, 81, 87, 89, 102, 119, 120,
  125-6
  fall of 21, 35-7 *passim,* 55, 124
  threats to 38, 46, 92, 97
  weakness of 4, 6, 126-7, 140
'stop-go' 87-9 *passim*
Strachey, Joe St Loe 50
*Sunday Mirror* 113
*Sunday Times* 39
Sweden 48, 115
Switzerland 55, 115
Swinton, Viscount 71

tariffs 52, 58, 69
  protectionist 16
taxation 70, 72, 102-3, 120, 121, 122,
  125, 134, 135
Thatcher, Margaret 45, 136, 141
three-day week 90, 100, 105
*Times, The* 20, 69, 132, 136-7
trade 49, 56, 58-9, 69, 70, 72, 78, 79, 99,
  101-2, 106, 140
Trade Union and Labour Relations Act
  120
Trades Union Congress 36, 47, 113-14,
  117, 119-20, 131
  Research Unit 120-21
trades unions 21, 34-5, 80, 90, 107,
  113-14, 116-17, 119, 120-21, 126, 132,
  134-6 *passim,* 142-3

149